24 HOUR RENEWAL HOTLINE 0845 607 6119

www.cornwall.gov.uk/library

one and all onen hag oll

First published 2012 by Fast-Print Publishing of Peterborough,
England.

www.fast-print.net/store.php

Man and Beast
Copyright © Noel Stuart 2012

ISBN: 978-178035-373-9

An environmentally friendly book printed and bound in England by
www.printondemand-worldwide.com

This book is made entirely of chain-of-custody materials

DEDICATION

I never realised initially "It's a Dog's Life" went so well. Since that time I am constantly encouraged to produce a sequel. This is it. Perhaps there is a gift in laughing at myself because many people have stopped me in the street to ask about the next book.

Of course my utmost thanks are due to Margaret, my wife, for her quiet encouragement, to my daughter, Kate for geeing me up during mental block moments and committing that unforgiveable crime of laughing at me in my moments of seriousness.

My proof readers-Margaret, Kate, Doreen Dowds and most of all Mike Hales, who excels at the job all deserve special mention, as like many writers who get too close to their work I can't they can't see the wood for the trees.

Mike Carter (www.digitalimagery.biz) has once more done a marvellous job on arranging the outer cover. My clients and patients have been my main inspiration as also have the readers of my book.

You may find it a bit strange having Chapter 50 at the start. However this is the last chapter of 'It's a Dog's Life' and links the two books

At two p.m. on Thursday afternoon, Brian and I were due at the Cooill Smithy to trim a bull's feet in preparation for the show season. Arthur Caley, at Ballabooie was a meticulous man and everything had to be exact in the show ring. This included his Aberdeen Angus bull, with which he intended to walk away with the 'best in show' rosette.

He was a large, gentle bull who was more at home sniffing daisies than being belligerent. He took his time about doing everything, including fathering the herd. Why bother rushing about the place like those artificial inseminator chaps who were trying to undercut his services? He knew his entire harem by name and kept them contented.

He had very aptly been christened "Traa-dy-Liooar!" which translated from the Manx (for the "come overs") means "Time Enough!"

Because he regarded exercise as an over rated pastime, his feet and toes had all overgrown until they curled up like a ram's horns.

The cattle truck arrived on time and Arthur led him out happily enough into the paddock behind the smithy. In retrospect we could probably have tied him up to a ring in the smithy and lifted his feet up one at a time. This wasn't good enough for Arthur who wanted the deluxe treatment for his pride and joy.

Once in the paddock we cast him; using Reuff's method. This consisted of a thirty-foot rope; with a loop around his neck continuing to a second loop about his chest and a third turn around his belly. I was delegated the privilege of holding the bullring whilst three men pulled on the rope at the rear.

Looking rather bewildered at the whole procedure "Traa-dy-liooar" subsided gracefully to the ground, as the loop tightened about his abdomen. We rolled his one-ton weight onto his side and tied his legs up with sidelines. I sat on his head and chatted to him whilst the blacksmith settled down to trim all his feet. It was an education to watch him working with hoof cutters, knives and rasp. His skill enabled him to have the feet looking shipshape in no time.

All this time the bull lay happily on the ground with me scratching his ear. I was so engrossed that I failed to notice signs of restlessness. Eventually, even his tolerance must have worn thin so he flexed his rather cramped muscles. The casting ropes snapped like sewing thread, I somersaulted up in the air as the bull stood up and all was chaos. Stories of bulls kneeling on their victim's chest, so that they were crushed like a hen's egg, flashed across my mind. A very rapid word with my maker and I opened my eyes to look straight into those of "Traa-dy-Liooar" who looked almost apologetic for disturbing me. Everyone else was too busy laughing to come to my rescue as I stood up and dusted myself off, as the bull meekly followed his master into the cattle truck.

The decreasing numbers of farm workers during the post war years had forced farmers to adapt their husbandry techniques. All stock were reared more intensively and batches of cattle were fed from the same trough. Horn damage became a problem, as in the excitement of feeding time they could readily damage another animal's eyes. Cows were crowded together to await milking and inevitably disputes would arise. Attempting to suture a wounded udder from which milk was pouring is a thankless occupation as many of the wounds did not heal correctly.

Dehorning cows and removing the horn buds from calves was becoming of economic importance due to damage from fighting and feeding in cramped conditions. Dehorning was certainly altering the problem of bullying in herds where the cow with the most effective horns became the herd boss and could keep the others away from the feeding trough.

I called at Michael Kennaugh's farm up above Ballawilleykilley near Union Mills to check up on several lame ewes. I didn't really expect to find him in the yard as he was probably out doing fieldwork. Every spare minute of his day was occupied profitably as he was constantly chasing his dream of more acres to pass on to his two sons, who were still at school in Douglas. Normally, he left the sheep in a pen for me to deal with on my own.

My car roared into the yard in a cloud of smoke as I had left my exhaust perched on a rock in the middle of his lane. I saw Mike sitting on a straw bale outside the calf pen looking somewhat shaken and exhausted.

"What's the problem, Mike?" I said as I wound down the car window. He was normally fairly active and robust.

"Well, Ned," he said despairingly. "Everyone is talking about disbudding calves at the moment, so I thought that I would have a go. I was lent an electric debudding iron and some local anaesthetic by my brother-in-law who told me how to do it. I have now upset the calf and exhausted myself trying to do the job. No more disbudding for me."

"You mean old devil," I said, slightly irritated at his lack of thought for the animal and determined to make him see the error of his ways. "You've been trying to save a few pennies by cutting corners and not really knowing where to inject the anaesthetic. As a result you've caused the calf a lot of pain and you look pretty knackered as well! It's easy if you use the anaesthetic properly. Let me give you a demonstration!"

"Now, if you disbud the calves fairly young you have very little trouble. You and brother-in-law can help each other out."

I showed him how to hold the calf whilst I injected the anaesthetic around the nerves supplying the horn area. "Now leave it for a few minutes whilst we have a look at the sheep and sort out their problems and by that time the whole area will be numb."

Shortly afterwards we returned to the pen. "Now the disbudding iron is hot I can burn away all the horn growing tissue around the base of the horn, leaving a small hole, in the skin, that heals very rapidly. Because the anaesthetic was injected in the correct spot she has felt nothing and stood perfectly still, making life easier for both of you. Let's get hold of another one and you can have a go whilst I show you where to inject the anaesthetic."

After we had finished disbudding half a dozen calves he was becoming very competent at the operation. As a result of this helping hand we were soon inundated with other requests to demonstrate the technique.

Whilst we worked with the calves our conversation turned to the sheep and Michael mentioned that he had received a good tip from Rodie Tait, the hill shepherd at Kate's Cottage. Whenever he had a ewe that would not allow a lamb to suckle, he would bring a strange dog into the pen. Immediately, the maternal instincts would take over as she defended the lamb, and afterwards she would accept it readily.

I collected Mary Sutherland from the airport the following Friday evening. She was coming over for a job interview to ease the pressure as we were so busy. After working in equine practice in Yorkshire she felt that she needed a change of direction. She was staying the night with Brian as they intended to exercise the horses early next morning.

She was much more attractive and mature than I remembered. Very confident in herself she had overcome her original air of shyness. Perfect teeth and auburn hair enhanced her attractive smile.

We started where we left off four years ago, enjoying each other's company and by the time we arrived at the surgery much of the Island gossip had been considered and I knew that we could work together as colleagues. The gossip network in the island was already buzzing at the sight of the vetinry driving around with a pretty young girl in his car!

The next evening we spent a very enjoyable few hours together having a splendid meal at the Carrick Bay Hotel in Port St. Mary. We had been given the centre table by the window, which overlooked the bay. The tide was full and the wavelets sparkled in the evening sun, as couples strolled slowly along the promenade, determined to take in all the pleasures of their holiday. As we sat drinking our coffee, watching the lights coming on across the bay, Brian arranged that Mary would join us in a month's time.

Little did we realise the repercussions that would arise from this pleasant evening and the manner in which it would shape our future.

Mary Sutherland drew the curtains of her bedroom to let the early morning sun pour in through the lattice. The sunbeams danced across the room embracing the drifting dust particles in this small cosy room, which had been her domain since childhood. Butterflies cavorted in her tummy as she regarded the room with it's pretty floral wallpaper and matching bedspread. The walls and level spaces were covered with trophies and ribbons from her show jumping career. In pride of place was a photograph of 'Minstrel', her feisty little pony who had danced through most of the show jumping rings in West Yorkshire.

Today was the start of her next big adventure in life. After three years in equine practise she realised that she was not truly one of the horsey set. As a child she had accompanied her farrier father everywhere. The glamour of the hunting and racing crowd had initially impressed but this specialised life soon paled when compared with the satisfaction of mixed practice.

When she was invited to join the practice in the Isle of Man with Brian Scanlon and Ned Carson, she leapt at the opportunity. She had spent many happy times there as a student and missed the omniprescence of the sea.

Hastily gathering her possessions together she descended into the kitchen to bid her parents a tearful farewell as she must hurry to board the afternoon boat at Liverpool. The sky was clear but she had a niggle at the back of her mind that the weather forecast had announced that it would deteriorate and she was not a natural sailor. The early morning shipping forecast had said something about barometric pressure 990 over Biscay dropping very rapidly to 955 with hurricane force winds. The scant knowledge she had of weather forecasting didn't tell her much but it inferred that there might be trouble ahead. As she headed westwards in her aged Hillman, clouds started to pile up on the horizon and rain beat fiercely upon the windscreen. Following a lunch break to consume her mother's lovingly prepared sandwiches, Mary arrived at the Pierhead in Liverpool and joined the boarding queue. She drove onto the "King Orry" the pride of the Manx Steam Packet and then disappeared into a deck cabin to endure the five hour journey to Douglas.

The Sea Gods were not very happy and greeted Mary's invasion of their island with the contempt reserved for mere mortals. All was well until the ship crossed the Mersey bar, when she was hit broadside on by a wild Sou'easterly gale. The equinox had arrived in force. The ship bravely nosed into the rolling seas, plunging into the troughs with the waves creaming across the fore and aft decks. Before mounting the heaving crest, the sturdy vessel shuddered her way forwards and then crashed into the next trough. The Irish sea was confirming it's reputation as the choppiest crossing in Europe and like many passengers on board the "King Orry" she contemplated a thermos flask of tea whilst her mind raced into all the techniques to prevent "mal de mer". Eventually, she settled on a comment from Ned, who had braved this journey many times. "If I feel queasy, I always go for'ard and face straight into the storm so as to get rid of the smell of oil and kippers. I find that I'm so busy trying to stand up that I forget about seasickness. I get rather wet but it's worth it in the long run."

Clambering onto the boat deck, she clung desperately to the superstructure and wondered how her beloved car was faring down below and hoping that the crew had lashed it down firmly. It would be a crying shame if some of it's rather antique paintwork became damaged before arrival. After half an hour of self discipline on deck she felt very damp but much better and staggered around the prostrate bodies of the few people laid out along the deck seating. Once inside her cabin she managed to drink a cup of tea to get some warmth in her body before once more heading onto the deck for fresh air and sea spray. Only three more hours to go she thought and I can have a warm bath!

After several hours of heavy seas, grey skies and horizontal rain she asked one of the Steam Packet crew if they had any idea of the time of arrival in Douglas. "Sorry, miss but the weather is too wild to berth in Douglas at present so we are heading South around the Calf of Man to get into the lee of the land. If conditions are right we shall probably drop anchor off Peel for a few hours until the storm abates. As the ship sailed up past Port Erin the seas subsided but, having found sanctuary, it looked as if they had a long and dreary wait ahead.

They hove too off Peel, and the ship came to life in the calm sea as a few rather subdued figures started to shuffle around the decks. It was a strange sensation to lie off shore watching the lights of the city that she knew so well but being unable to berth in the small harbour and found herself wondering which lights might be from Ned and Moira's house. Would they be looking out of the window and asking themselves if she was sitting on board or prostrate in her cabin. Feeling quite peckish she went off to the buffet for a tray of tea and sandwiches to sustain her until landing. It was very warm on board so she nodded off in the cabin in exhausted sleep only to be aroused four hours later as the "King Orry" once again rounded the southern tip of the island, but into much calmer seas. They docked at the Victoria pier in Douglas six hours late and very weary. Brian had come down to meet her with the news that she was staying with them for the night and that Ruth, the housekeeper had prepared a meal for her.

Ruth the house keeper had been rushing about like a broody hen all evening and welcomed her at the door, insisting that she sat in front of a blazing fire with a bowl of soup and a glass of warming drink. Mary was cloaked in a relaxing warmth and fatigue started to creep over her to such an extent that she found her attention wandering. Ruth took her upstairs to her room where she collapsed into the soft embrace of a feather bed with a hot water bottle. She only had time to count one sheep before sleep crept over her.

A sharp knock at the door announced the arrival of another day, in another life. Ruth walked into the bedroom with a mug of tea and drew back the bedroom curtains to admit the start of a glorious bright day. "Here you are Mary. It doesn't do to lie in bed after nine o'clock. I thought that once we had some breakfast you could be mucking out Baska ,the horse, and then you and I could go out on exercise. Don't think about work today. We have fixed up lodgings for you, in Westmoreland Road, with a lovely widow, Mrs Callow. You will probably want to go and settle in after lunch."

Mrs Callow was very welcoming and her Border Collie, Madge, made a great fuss of the newcomer, whilst the smug black cat on the settee opened one eye, summed up the situation and went back to sleep. "You must be very tired after the journey," commenced Mrs Callow. "The boat isn't normally that late arriving. I'll make a nice cup of tea and we can sit down and get to know each other before the evening meal. My family used to farm up in Maughold until my dear husband, George, was killed by his own bull ten years ago. They were great companions until one day the bull, 'Izzy', felt a bit skittish and knocked him down and killed him. Little did he know that his enormous weight would crush my dear George."

"Fortunately", she continued, "I am very blessed in having my son Tom, who lives at home. Although sometimes I think that I run a teahouse for him and his friends. He's the fisheries officer for the Board of Agriculture and has a very busy life. You may call me Jenny and I shall call you Mary!"

"We have our evening meal at about six o'clock when he arrives back from work. I can see that we shall have to make allowances for you if you are out on call. I can always put your meal in the oven and stick a plate over it. Tom should be back in a few minutes. He's been playing rugger against the Southern Young Farmers club this afternoon. It's all part of a charity fund-raising day."

By five o'clock Mary had finished her unpacking and was settling down in the sitting room to relax with a book. When the door opened to reveal a well built young man with blond, curly hair. He must have been well over six feet in height and had a broad cherubic smile on his face. "Welcome" he greeted her. "I'm Tom. You must be Mary. I was expecting a lady vet to be large and muscular to cope with the farm stock but here you are as slim as a rush and much too attractive to be mixing with rough old farmers!"

"Don't believe it," replied Mary, laughing. "I've been able to cope with farm work in the Yorkshire dales for a few years without coming to harm. I did get a bit overwhelmed by the horsey set and was delighted when Mr Scanlon invited me back. I saw practice here as a student and fell for the island and it's people."

Tom chuckled. "Their loss is our gain, methinks! Come to think of it, I shall be secretary of Young Farmers Club next year. How about joining us? We have a lot of fun and it's the best marriage bureau in the Island."

"Hold on!" cried Mary. "Here I am, just arrived in the Island and you have me in YFC and half way up the aisle already. I was a YFC member for several years until my work took over. The answer to your first comment is 'perhaps' and to the second I might even have a wealthy landowner already seeking my hand, so any suitors must try pretty hard."

"I can see that we shall get on very well," laughed Tom, joining in the verbal jousting. "I've met my match but watch out for those guys in the rugger club."

At that moment Jenny walked in to announce supper. "Thomas, did I hear you teasing this poor young lady, when she has just set foot on the Island. Can you not give her a bit of peace?" Tom put his arms around Jenny in a great bear hug. "Hush now mother. He retorted. "You're too quick off the mark and interrupted us just as I was offering my hand in marriage."

"Oh! I apologise for this idiot son of mine, Mary. I've a good mind to send him off to bed with no supper!"

"Please forgive him", said Mary, with tears of laughter streaming down her face. "I was only practising my instant seduction technique and he fell for it! I shall treat him more gently in future!"

"Will the two of you sit down to your meal before I turn you both out, exclaimed Jenny, in exasperation. " There's a nice warm fire next door if you want to rest this evening. You'll have a very busy day ahead of you tomorrow Mary. Just settling in and finding where everything is."

As Mary slipped into bed later in the evening she was blissfully happy with her new friends and, fortunately, was unable to see into the future!

The first day in a new practice can often be very daunting and guaranteed to have a degree of chaos for all concerned.

Mary arrived at the surgery at 8 a.m., ready to organise her gear in Matilda, her well-used Hillman. She worked on the premise that if she ran it into the ground whilst being paid a mileage allowance they would both benefit.

Brian and Ned were sitting in the kitchen planning the day ahead. "Welcome Mary," said Brian. "Pull up a chair and we can discuss the day over a cup of tea. There are already calls in and Ned has a TB test first thing. We thought that as you are the first lady vet in the Island that we would not throw you to the lions too soon. We have no problems with your capabilities but some of the older farmers are very conservative. To the extent that one old boy said to me last week, 'Don't send any young girl in to do a calving-they're not made for it. I send my wife indoors when such things happen!' So you may have the odd problem."

Ned brought over a mug of steaming tea. "We have paved the way for you by putting a short article in the Isle of Man Times that we are employing the first lady vet in the Island who has had vast experience in horse and farm practice and it seems to have gone down very well, particularly with the Young Farmers Club."

At this stage Mary smiled and couldn't resist repeating her little bit of repartee with Tom Callow. "I eventually had to admit to his mother that he had proposed to me."

"Well done," chuckled Ned. "I can see that you have got his measure although he probably fancies you! I was just getting on to the second part of our Mary sales campaign. Why not join the YFC. It would be a good way to get to know the farms and become accepted by the farmers."

Brian continued. "We felt that for a day or two it would help you to get your bearings if you came around with each of us in turn. What do you think to that idea? And for a few days you can be accompanied by Alan Ramsden our manager who probably knows more about the practice than we do."

"Excellent," she replied. "It will give me a few days to stock up my car with drugs and equipment. Where can I get boots and protective clothing?"

"We have that all arranged for you, assured Brian. "We hope that you won't be too proud to call us for help or advice at any time of the day or night. The farmers will respect you for it. It certainly worked very well when Ned joined me. Now it only remains for you to accompany me on the morning round and let Ned get on with his test. I suggest that we call in at the market and get you a pair of boots and a dustcoat to protect your clothes."

"But," said Mary, hesitantly. "I thought that you were working and I was sight-seeing today."

"Well," continued Brian, breaking into his Ulster brogue, which was accentuated when he was enjoying himself or being particularly devious. "I was not being quite exact with you but it should be good fun. After all you're a dab hand with horses which we are going to see first. Hurry up now!"

Mary looked pleadingly at Ruth and waved her hands in the air as she moved towards the door. "Is he always mysterious like this?"

Ruth just smiled quietly because she had guessed what was coming. "Mr Scanlon, don't forget this wee parcel that I made up for you! I shall expect you both back for lunch mind."

As they drove off Brian commenced, "Our first call, is to see a lame horse belonging to Col.

Charles De Vere Pullen. I told them that you were coming and were a very capable horse vet. His wife, Daphne, is a man-eater but don't worry, I have tamed her. She is a very capable horse woman. They arrived over here from Leicestershire a few years ago and are trying to organise a drag hunt as we don't have any foxes in the Island."

"We are approaching 'Ballakilley' now so I shall pull in here. If you would care to drive the car I shall sit in the passenger seat." At this point he unwrapped Ruth's mystery parcel, pulled out a sling and rested his right arm in it. "It works wonders sometimes if I can't handle an animal. You will be accepted as the resident expert, under my guidance."

Mary looked at Brian quite sharply. "Isn't that cheating your client?" "God forbid," responded Brian, eyes twinkling. "This should help your self-confidence and keep the man-eater at bay. Here we are at the gate so try to smile."

Arriving in the yard, they were met by Col Pullen, who was just leaving the tack room. "Good morning Brian. Sorry to hear that your arm is out of commission. I hope that you're fighting fit soon as Jane Cathcart is coming over in a couple of weeks and no doubt you will be dining with her!"

After a slight pause and avoiding the comment Brian said, in a slightly strained voice. "Charles, may I introduce Mary Sutherland, who has just joined the practice. She has been working in equine practice in Yorkshire. I have asked her if she will stand in for me today"

"Delighted to meet you," continued Charles, "It's lovely to see a new face. Oh! Here's Daphne, just arrived in time to meet Miss Sutherland, the new assistant in the practice."

"Good morning Miss Sutherland," said Daphne. "Delighted to meet a young lady with your reputation as a horse vet."

Mary gaped in surprise. "Don't look so surprised," she continued. "When I heard that you were coming I 'phoned an old friend of ours, Brigadier Heveningham, who told me that you were extremely capable. And pretty too! I think, Brian, that young Jane will have some competition eh!"

Brian looked quite abashed and said nothing! At this stage Mary didn't know what to say so interjected with "Shall we look at the lame filly, Mrs Pullen. What is the history?"

"Silly little thing. A bit skittish and has probably only twisted her fetlock. I have her in the loosebox."

As they entered the box Mary lifted the foreleg of 'Fly by Night', the filly. Palpating the tendons and fetlock didn't evince too much discomfort until she reached the bulb of the heel, which was red and swollen. "Here's her problem. She's trodden on a blackthorn which is still in the heel. After I've removed it and given her penicillin and anti tetanus serum. I should like you to warm bathe it twice daily and report back in two days time."

"Thank you Miss Sutherland for a good diagnosis. And Brian! I do hope that you improve quickly for my guest in two weeks time," concluded Daphne with a smile flickering across her face.

As they drove away Brian had a smile on his face to indicate a job well done. Mary stared at him fixedly. "That was a bit hard on a new assistant but I must confess it worked well, particularly as Daphne had already checked up on me."

"It is often a useful ploy," chuckled Brian, trying to keep a straight face. We have another one later so be prepared. I thought that you handled her extremely well. We call her the Brigadier because she barks out commands to the Colonel!"

"If I'm not being too intrusive, who is the mysterious visitor for whom you should be prepared? It all sounds very intriguing to me. You went very quiet!"

23

"Only a friend from Melton, who visits the Island on occasion. We have common interests." replied Brian rather testily in a tone that indicated the end of the conversation.

Mary hugged herself inside as she had the mischievous thought that even Brian appeared to have an Achille's Heel. He had won the first round today, but there would be lots of other opportunities.

"Now I'm going to give you the opportunity to prove yourself against a real tough nut. He was a bit hard on Ned when he first arrived. You'll know that you've succeeded if he doesn't order you off the farm. Jack Comish, at Ballavaish, doesn't suffer fools gladly. He reckons that he has had to fight against the elements and his fellow man all his life."

"I should be frightened to death of this man but I feel that you are trying to wind me up Brian," muttered Mary, trying to keep her eyes on the road and listen to his comments. "If he's that bad maybe I should go home!"

"Och," replied Brian, "Maybe he'll be easy on you. Drive straight through Castletown, up the hill, turn left down the lane and we're there. I do hope he's in a good mood!"

As they drove into the yard Jess the collie greeted them and dropped a stone on Mary's foot-ready for a game. After a couple of throws for the dog, Jack appeared out of the shippon and strode across the yard to meet them. "Good morning Brian. What have you been doing with your arm in a sling-did you come off the horse? Introduce me to your secretary, yessir!"

"'Morning Jack. It's nothing really. I think that my arm will be better very soon. Let me introduce you to our new colleague Mary Sutherland. I felt that I should bring her round to see some of our better clients for her first couple of days. She'll probably find us a bit quiet over here as she is used to dealing with wild stock on the Yorkshire dales. Just as well since I am incapacitated. What's the problem?"

"With all due respects Miss I think that this could be too heavy for you. I have a cow very lame in the back foot and I find it hard to lift up!"

"Don't worry Mr Comish," replied Mary, smiling disarmingly at him. "I'll just collect the gear from the car and you and I should manage her fairly well." Off she went to the car and returned with a length of rope and a leather case of tools.

"Now, I shall put a loop of rope around her leg, above the hock. We'll throw the other end over the beam and back under the leg. As you are the strong one, you pull on the rope and lift her leg in the air."

Wielding a curved foot knife Mary continued, "Now I can examine the foot in comfort and scrape it out with a foot knife. Look here! There's a puncture wound through the sole. I shall pare it away to get some drainage and - lo and behold!- stinking black pus is oozing out. You can let the rope go now and I shall inject her. It looks as if she has stood on a nail in the yard. Can you put her foot into a pail of water with Epsom salts for a couple of days and she should be all right."

"Thank you Miss," expostulated Jack. "I'm very impressed and must apologise for doubting you. It looks as if I've been a bit careless with nails around the yard. I hope that Jess didn't upset you by dropping stones on your feet. That's a sign that she likes you!"

As they drove away from the farm Mary commented tersely, "Are you happy now Brian after this morning's work?"

"Och! Of course I am," he replied. "I knew that you'd have no problems dealing with them. They are both very pleased with you."

"No, it's not so much the reaction of the clients I was thinking about, but advice I received from you as a student. Do you recall that we had a very earnest discussion about the difference between the veterinary science and the veterinary art and the importance of them both in general practice! That made me think very deeply about my course in life. Did I want to enter the hurly burly of practice or to join into government service. But to do the civil service thing you have to speak their own jargon full of acronyms and cliches, which are meaningless to we poor mortals. Alternatively, I could have gone into research or a veterinary teaching post."

"So you settled for the rigours of practice Mary. Why?" said Brian, full of interest.

"I debated the subject with my fellow students," continued Mary. "First of all we looked at the students in our years, who excelled academically. Most of them we could not have worked with in practice, because they were too intelligent to talk at a layman's level and did not have a basic humility. Government service meant selling your soul to the politicians. The third group of teachers and researchers are indispensable but the majority had not been in practice for long enough to be able to apply their vast knowledge practically. Those of us who entered into practice did so because it is a people based career not an academic exercise"

"Mary! You've put it very well. Would you mind pulling in here at the Jolly Farmer. I shall remove my sling and offer you a drink, whilst I talk to George Andrews, a farm manager about his cow."

George saw them as they entered and after a brief introduction set to and reported on his lame cow's progress. "It's doing fine now, thanks Mr Scanlon. Glad to see that you are feeling better. The grapevine reported that you had a badly broken arm! I suppose the next thing is we shall be seeing Miss Sutherland on the farm. I shall have to talk to John Broughton. As you know he can be funny with new faces.

Having sorted out the cow's problem with George, Brian brought up the subject of the veterinary art again. "So you think that the veterinary art is very much the equivalent of a doctor's bedside manner!" George commented.

"Quite right," was Mary's immediate response. "It covers many things -humility, the ability to chat with your animal and client, a deep, caring outlook and, above all a joy in your work. If you lose any of those you have problems. I'm eternally grateful to Brian for his advice when I was a student."-

"Happen, you've hit the nail on the head," chimed in George. "Those are the factors that I respect in my vet. He doesn't have to know everything so long as he's understanding and practical. You can come to our place anytime."

Listening to this banter and the results of a day's work, Brian realised that Mary could hold her own in a man's world and that we were lucky to have her help.

5

I arrived in the office next morning to find a full complement of staff. Mary was bubbling with pleasure. "It's your turn to draw the short straw today, Ned! I'm coming with you as a passenger as Brian's sprained shoulder has miraculously recovered. I feel that it's in anticipation of his guest"

I looked a bit confused but felt that it was time to depart as Brian was getting a bit agitated again. "Not another lady," I said, enjoying his discomfiture. "Is this part of the veterinary art which seems to fascinate the opposite sex?" At this stage Brian gave a snort and disappeared into the surgery in search of peace.

As we got into the car I gave a resumé of the morning's work. "We are going to see a pony for Meg McCall, a lovely redhead, who has ponies in Maughold. After that a couple of cows to dehorn for Jim Moore in Ballaugh. He's a bit rough and ready but honest as can be. After that we have to castrate a few calves for Roy Callin. Keep your wits about you when you're on the farm as he's got quite a reputation as a leg puller. How do you feel about dehorning and castration? "

"After yesterday," she replied smiling, "It should be plain sailing. I'm quite happy about castrations. How do you dehorn cows? I have always used embryotomy wire with special handles. A bit tiring as I don't have a bulky physique.

Who is this mysterious visitor that is due to stay with the De Vere Pullens in the next few weeks? Brian seems to get quite excited when she is mentioned."

"I'm not very sure Mary. As you realise he's a chick magnet! He has this fatal fascination for the female of the species and is constantly having to fight a rearguard action when they become too serious. I keep getting caught up trying to extricate him from his amours! Why? Are you interested?"

"Of course not!" she retorted defensively. "Not my type. I'm looking for someone younger and athletic like yourself but I don't suppose that Moira would hand you over."

"Here we are. A quick look over the bridge to check for sea trout and down the lane to see Meg."

I could see a dark shape lying in the overhang of the bridge and undulating gently in the current. It looks promising, maybe I could have a bit of sport here next week.

I drove into the yard to find Meg grooming a pony in the yard. It was a lovely picture as she worked in the warmth of the sun in the cobbled yard.

"Morning Meg! I've brought an expert with me this morning. Meet Mary Sutherland, who has just joined us."

Wiping her hands on her dustcoat Meg walked across and greeted Mary. "Delighted to meet you Mary. These men have given you a great write-up in the papers. You couldn't have joined a nicer practice."

"Thanks Meg. What's the problem today."

"I'm a bit concerned about 'Starlight', who has had a runny nose with a bit of a cough for a few days. Do you think that she might be starting off with strangles? Also, 'Danny', the gelding, seems to be itching a bit."

Very carefully, Mary examined 'Starlight' and checked her throat glands and nostrils after listening to her lungs. She looks all right to me- not strangles-probably just a cold. I'll give her a course of antibiotics and she should be fine. Can I see 'Danny'?"

'Danny' was looking rather moth-eaten where he had been rubbing and itching against the side of the loosebox. "Look here," said Mary, parting the hair on his neck these silvery things are 'nits' - louse eggs. They are smart enough to stick their eggs to the hairs. I can almost feel myself itching a bit. They may have been worrying you. I can let you have a wash for his coat. Repeat it in ten days. Lots of grooming and wash the tools separately. It's a pity that hens aren't that smart. Just imagine picking their eggs off a fence!"

"You've relieved my mind, Mary. Yes, I have been a bit scratchy of late." At that moment a ship's siren sounded at sea. Instantly, Meg said goodbye and rushed up the yard to pull her scarlet nightshirt up the flagstaff.

"Let's go," I said, "That is Meg's love song for her husband, who is first mate on the Manx boat. Once the siren sounds all is forgotten. Now we must head for Ballaugh"

Old Jim Moore was a cattle dealer, who lived in a roadside cottage just beside Ballaugh Bridge. He only kept a few stock nowadays as his time was taken up caring for Martha, his wife, who was crippled with rheumatism. With the aid of a stick he hobbled out of his cottage to greet us. "Nice to have a sight on you Mr Carson. Who's this sprightly filly you've got with you. Enough to make my blood flow faster Miss! Don't take any notice of me Miss-I'm a cantankerous old bugger really. I've got the two young heifers tied up in the shippon. Bought them in Ramsey mart just last week. They seem to fetch a better price without horns. Somethin' to do with feeding in outdoor racks they tell me! Mind you the margins is small so don't charge me too much."

"Don't you worry Mr Moore. We'll look after your finances although you're probably related to the rich folks at St Johns Mill. You may as well come into the shippon and watch Miss Sutherland take the horns off one heifer and I'll deal with the other. "

I held the heifer, whilst Mary very rapidly removed her horns using a butcher's saw. Inevitably, we hit a small artery which jetted blood across the shed and sprinkled liberally over Jim's thatch of tousled silver hair. "Steady on miss. What'll my Martha say when I go into the house covered in blood. She's not used to things like this. She's a fine lady! Not used to rough old country folk like me. Her father was a draper up in Ramsey but for some strange reason she fancied me. Mind you, I was a tall young man - rather fancied by many of the girls in the Young Farmers. Always came first in the sheaf pitchin' contest at inter club sports."

I dehorned the next heifer fairly easily as Mary had held her firmly with the nose grips. "It always makes me sweat a bit if you have twenty or thirty to dehorn in one operation. I'm hoping to try this new plaited wire instead of a saw next time. It seems to cut very well and isn't so tiring to use."

As we cleaned up after the operation I commented to Mary. "The critical factor with dehorning is to prevent bleeding. Tie a ligature of binder twine around the head to act as a ligature. If the animals are being fed from a hayrack put a swab over the wound to stop hayseeds dropping in to the wound."

It's time that we went on to see Roy and Val at Lhergy Dhoo. If you pass the Roy Callin test you should be able to cope with any of our clients. They're both inclined to tease a bit so be careful."

At that moment the phone rang indoors and Jim came hobbling out. "It's for you Mr Carson. Good thing I caught yer' It's that Ruth from the office wants to speak to you urgent like!" I went indoors and greeted Martha, who held the phone out to me. "What's the problem Ruth?"

"Ned! We have a bit of a problem. You know Mr Kaighin up at Cronk-y-Voddy. The one that gets upset easy. He's just sent the men from the Board of Agricultue off the premises again. He must have been a bit agitated as he was waving a shotgun in the air. Fortunately, there is no problem at the moment but Duggie Kerruish says that you and he get on well together and asked if you would call in to see him and calm down the situation."

"Don't worry Ruth!. We shall attack him in his castle and anyway I can always hide behind Mary! If we don't return, send out a search party or even better suggest that Duggie sends out Josie Corkish, the Board of Agriculture secretary, to confront him. That should send him scuttling for cover," I concluded, chuckling at the thought of five feet nothing of Josie facing down the wild man of the mountains.

As we drove along towards Kirk Michael, I related the tale of Ronnie Kaighin to Mary. "He's not a bad old boy really, when you understand him and realise what he's come through. He comes from an old farming family who have always worked hard to scratch a living up in the hills. They were always so involved in the endless drudgery, labouring away on such poor land, that they never got away from the place. The only communication they had with other folk was the weekly service at the chapel at Cronk-y-Voddy. The odd trip into St John's Market with stock and eggs was like a holiday. Then they had to hurry back to father, who would smell their breath lest they had had a drink. 'Devil's Brew' he called it. If they wanted to visit relatives it was half a day's ride across the hills to Glen Roy above Laxey."

I stopped to show her the view as we climbed up the hill towards Little London. "At sunset there is a most beautiful view and the light is such that you feel that the Mull of Galloway and Ireland are only a stone's throw away. Now to return to Ronnie. He's not the most gifted of people and you might wonder whether he's the result of inbreeding, which was rife some years back, when people hardly ventured out of the parish for a bride. You will meet a lot of 'simpletons' on the farms still, but they play a useful part in the family, that is, if you don't upset them. He lives by himself on a small holding near Sartfell."

As we turned into the long narrow lane flanked by high hedges there was only the decor of Butterwort and Foxgloves to guide us away from the stone wall hidden beneath. I had numerous scratches on the cars bodywork to demonstrate the learning curve I had undergone. These tracks were built for cattle and pony and trap and not wide car bodies. The rough track was full of ruts and potholes to test the unwary. The huddle of greystone buildings with a few wind-bent hawthorns growing out of the hedge, stood out against the skyline as we reached an old age-rusted gate blocking our way.

"This is your gate Mary! It only has one hinge and watch the nettles, although I do have a homoeopathic cure if you are stung!"

Ever willing, Mary leapt out and as she swung the gate aside a pair of border collies ran around the corner barking a greeting. I drove into the cobbled yard as Ronnie came out of the cowhouse with a hayfork in hand and a scatteration of hens, protesting loudly. ran up onto the dung heap.

He must have given a good impression to Mary, his hair sticking out wildly from under an old battered cap, a khaki shirt rolled up to the elbows and black, rough trousers held up with binder cord at the top and with sacking tied around his legs above heavy black boots.

"Afternoon Ronnie! How are you keeping? Can I introduce Mary Sutherland to you! She has just joined the practice and as we were passing I thought to call in on you. You see she is keen on trout fishing and I wanted to show her the little pond that we've built on your stream."

"Mighty nice to have a sight at yer Mr Carson! Of course the young lady can have a look at our pond and fish in it if she wants. I didn't knaw that they 'ad wimmen as vetinries. Aw'right for cats and dogs I suppose but they wouldn't be able to handle stock!"

"Beware Ronnie! You could be in for a big surprise. For the last three years she's been calving cows and dehorning bullocks. By the way have you got any rabbits. My wife loved the last ones you gave her. If you ever want rabbit stew Mary, Ronnie always has some fresh ones. He's the best rabbit catcher this side of the Point of Ayre! What did I hear about the Board of Agriculture man upsetting you?"

"Oh! That were nathing Mr Carson- just some snotty nosed little twirp throwin' his weight around. Mind you I sent him off pretty quick. He didn't knaw nothin' about his job so I returned him home to his mammy! When he told me that he'd never looked after sheep I reckoned that he shouldn' be advisin' me on lookin' after mine!"

"I know what you mean Ronnie. Be a bit careful next time or they might take your gun away and that would upset your rabbiting. If you get a problem like that give Duggie Kerruish or myself a ring and we can help to sort it out. I could do with a couple of your rabbits!"

As we bumped down the track away from the farm towards the road Mary sat silently beside me, looking thoughtful. Now, I have always found that a woman who looks inscrutable is unnerving, almost scary. As if they are reading your thoughts. I'm all for a bit of idle banter so I pulled the car in at the roadside and said casually. "Penny for your thoughts! You're looking overcome with something!"

"Ned!" retorted Mary sharply, eyes flashing. "I'm not sure who you've been using the most for your own advantage, Ronnie or myself."

I was quite taken aback. Was I a manipulator of people? Then I realised that I had been controlling the situation in order to reach a happy ending. Please God! Don't let me become a wheedling and devious politician! "I'm very sorry if that's how it appears but as I know Ronnie's temperament well, I have to be a bit devious and keep him calm. He can break out in uncontrollable rages if he is backed into a corner and could cause great damage with anything from a hayfork to a shotgun. There are one or two others like him on the Island. I don't like confronting people in such situations. Much better to stand back and see the whole picture instead of being black and white on a problem. "

I added, rather lamely. "I felt that fishing ploy was a good introduction to make you acceptable as he loves anything to do with wildlife. Probably he'll offer to take you out fishing when you arrive on the farm." I couldn't help smiling at her look of consternation. "That little bit of gamesmanship is what I regard as the veterinary art and you did blush prettily when I said it."

"Do you remember the switchback road leading out to Knocksharry. Dad has his eye on a bungalow there as a retirement home. Just before we get there we are going to drop down into the yard at Lhergydhoo to check up on a calf for Roy Callin. He'll never forgive me if I don't introduce you. Here we are!"

The yard wasn't very posh as some farms go, but it was a hive of activity each morning as Roy and Beakie were up early milking the cows and, then Val would go off on the milk round to Peel. It always seemed to me that they never stopped.

It was getting on for lunchtime and Roy was cleaning up in the dairy. He appeared at the door, leaning on his broom. "My God Ned! Who's the fancy bit of stuff you've got here. I heard on the grapevine that you were getting help. Perhaps I should book her for a special consultation. How are yer doing! Mary is it?" Then turning towards the house, he shouted "Val! Look what I've found in the yard! Can we give her a good home?"

Eyes alight with laughter, Val appeared at the back door looking pretty as ever, her hair, black as a raven's wing compared to Mary's auburn locks. "Why hello! You'll be Mary! I'm surprised that you were sent out in the car alone with Ned. He's got an awful reputation as a womaniser. Roy, would you stop your teasin' yer randy old devil and leave the poor girl alone! Anyway your Dad is taking the calf to the mart, go and help him load it."

There was an old battered Ford Ten of uncertain vintage in the yard. It had started off life as a splendid black motor but had now developed a strange bluish tint on the paintwork as it aged. Roy and Alured, his father, came out of the shed carrying a young calf in a large hessian sack, tied around the neck. Roy pulled out the back seat and laid the calf inside on the floor and father drove off towards St Johns. As he drove out of the yard Alured, with a wicked twinkle in his eye leaned out of the window chuckling and said, "Welcome to Lhergy Dhoo, miss! I'm surprised that they let you out in the car alone with Ned. He's got an awful reputation!"

"There," commented Roy, "keeps father busy and it's a lot safer and cheaper than one of those big trucks owned by Leeces. Come in and have a cuppa, yessir, whilst we get to know this young lady."

"Hey Ned! Does Moira know that you're driving round the countryside with a young lady.and her expecting another youngster soon. It'll cost you a few pints to keep quiet"

"Shut up Roy! interjected Val. "If she ever comes here, I'll be watching you. I think that we could find a nice young man for her in the YFC."

"Hold on!" Mary broke in, eyes sparkling with laughter. "I met one on my first night here and he proposed to me before we were introduced. Anyway, Ned and I have known each other for a long time. He will tell you about it when you buy him a pint!"

Brian and I had arranged to meet at the Woodburn Hotel for a drink before going home.

Brian said, "I had a lady and her dog in surgery this afternoon Mary. She happened to mention that she is the widow of a vet who used to practice in Ayrshire. When I told her that we still don't charge veterinary families, policemen or priests she was absolutely delighted of course. Did you do this in Yorkshire."

"Yes!" She responded. "We have always been a Robin Hood practice and helped out the poor at the expense of the rich. The same fees for all is a bit hard. You can't charge an old penniless widow as you would a lawyer! Tell me do you permit your colleagues to tell tall stories to people like Ronnie Kaighin. It looks as if I will be expected to arrive on calls with a fishing rod in my hand."

Brian chortled into his pint. "Good for you Ned. I'm sure that they will make a nice couple when they walk down the aisle. Oh! I think that we can let you in gently in the morning, Mary. How about doing morning surgery and a couple of calls afterwards. In the next week or two we hope to have you TB testing. Then we shall brief you on the delectable Josie Corkish. Come to think of it, there is a test due at Peter Quirk's farm next week. It might broaden your education Mary.

"Brian" I continued. "Do you remember, Bronwyn Jones, that rather coquettish little Welsh girl, with the big blue eyes, who stole your heart last year. A good thing that she went back to Denbighshire. I was afraid you might have got involved with yet another attractive young thing as she kept asking about you."

Brian blushed and tried to ignore me as he avoided eye contact. "Oh! I recall her" he replied vaguely. "How on earth did she come to bring her dog into us?"

"Don't you remember?" I continued, glimpsing Mary, who had the hint of a smile on her face. "She came over to work during the summer and had brought her mongrel bitch with her. You treated her false pregnancy with stilboestrol tablets to get rid of the milk. Two weeks later she called again for a further course. That was the last we heard of her until the autumn until she wrote to us again, from Wales, for two more courses of those wonderful tablets. I did worry a little when she wrote to us again for a further course." By this time Brian was showing some concern and Mary had retreated to the corner to watch us sparring.

"This morning I had a phone call from Mick Laverty, who qualified with me. He lives in the same village as Bronwyn. She arrived on his doorstep yesterday waving our pill packet in the air. Could she have a couple of courses of the tablets as her bitch was in milk again. Mick insisted on examining the bitch and realised that there was no problem as there was a scar on her abdomen where she had been spayed recently. Bronwyn is notorious for seducing almost every

47

available young man. She must have heard that in the USA, during the war, this drug was originally used on several University campuses as "the morning after pill" for girls, who had been sleeping around. It worked like magic and prevented many pregnancies. It was also referred to as the Biological Time bomb, because many of the girls involved later married and had a family. A percentage of their female children developed cancer of the cervix as teenagers. I gather that Mick read her chapter and verse on the subject and sent her off to see her doctor, feeling a very chastened young lady."

Brian commented, "What a salutary story. I shall have to eschew all interest in the fairer sex. Have you heard anything about this Mary?"

"Yes! I have. There was an article in the New Scientist about it. It does make you worry about the side effects of some of the proprietary drugs. Come to think of it, we use digitalis for heart problems regularly but in spite of it being a potent poison our predecessors learnt to use it with safety, over many years, so we benefit from their errors in dosage. Oops! Look at the time. I must rush off for tea and Tom Callow has offered to take me to the Young Farmers meeting this evening. Bye!" Off she rushed with her auburn hair streaming in the sunshine.

As she disappeared out of the door Brian grinned and said, "Tom Callow won't know what's hit him if he hopes to keep up with that young lady!"

The truth of Brian's masked comment the previous evening came out next morning as I was answering the phone before my morning round.

8

I was chatting to a lady on the telephone one morning about vaccinating her pup. As I was talking I had heard a yelp and voices raised in concern from the waiting room. I put down the receiver as Brian came through with a white poodle in his arms. "I'll just put him in the kennel and we can repair his dislocation later on. I've known young Peter poodle for some time -a randy little devil who will travel miles after a pretty little bitch. Apparently he went out on the tiles last night and limped home early this morning. He must have been knocked over by a cyclist. Too busy dreaming of things that might have been! Thanks for answering the phone. Ruth has rushed off early to the butcher's for meat as I'm entertaining a young lady tonight."

"Oh! I said, probing gently," Anyone that I know. She's not Welsh by any chance?"

"No!" came the abrupt reply. "You're a true Manxman. You have lived in the island too long and are looking for a bit of gossip. What you don't know you make up. She is a mature and sensible young woman. Unmarried and living in Melton Mowbray. A different type completely from that Bronwyn. I just don't know what put it into your head that I was interested in her!"

"That makes a change," I replied, enjoying his discomfort. "I am only looking after your welfare as I would hate to see you pursued by a gold digger, and you've had too many flighty young fillies in your stable lately. Is she a horsewoman, coming from Melton?"

"Yes. I met her at the Quorn Hunt Ball last year. She's staying with the De Vere Pullens at Ballakilley. Now that the interrogation is over, perhaps we should get some work done. When we have a few minutes I should appreciate some assistance from Moira and yourself. We'll talk about it later."

"I know that you had planned to head out West. Could you take on the Northern route as I have a small problem to sort out? Anyway, Meg McCall up in Maughold has yet another lame pony to look. You know that she has taken a shine to you. I even suspect that she makes her horses lame just to see you!" finishing off with a delighted grin.

"Oh! I feel that I must give you some bad news. I heard that Graham and Vera Sutherland went their separate ways a couple of months ago. He had the call of the wild and has returned to Kenya as a district officer. Vera stayed in the Island but has disappeared from the social scene. She will probably surface amongst the Island's social elite! I'm sure that as a true Manxman you will soon flush her out."

"It's all very well for you!" I retorted. "I do all the donkey work tracking down the lady, and you practice your charms. Perhaps I should be charging agent's fees!"

As promised, I called in to have a word with Brian. He had been suffering with a nasty bout of laryngitis and, as well as feeling a bit under the weather had been left with a continuous rasping cough.

The facts eventually emerged that he wanted Moira and I to join him at a dance in The Castle Mona Hotel in a couple of weeks. "It is more as a chaperone really that I want your company. I have a problem coming up on the horizon, in the shape of Jane Cathcart. Did I tell you that I met her at the Quorn and Belvoir Hunt Ball last year, when I was staying with friends in Melton Mowbray? She is a gorgeous looking young lady, estranged from her husband, an officer in the Guards. It was a mutual attraction. She is very vivacious, a bit flighty like a yearling filly but fun to be with so we spent the whole week in each other's company. Unfortunately, it's getting a bit serious now and she keeps flying over to the Island to stay with the De Vere Pullens' and dragging me off to dinner parties. She's a wealthy, only child, who I suspect is using me as her latest plaything!"

Of course Moira and I were delighted to act as bodyguards, and looked forward to enjoying a good evening as well. We could never solve the mystery of Brian's instant atttraction for the opposite sex. I had put it down to overproduction of pheromones, that mysterious 'je ne sais quoi' that makes boy moths home in on lady moths. He was like a lighthouse drawing in helpless migratory birds except that in his case they all seemed to be predatory whilst he seemed to be naively indifferent to his allure.

Over the next few days I could see that he was down in the dumps, partly from his cold and partly the prospect of being steam-rolled by Jane. We met at the Jolly Farmer that evening and he told me that Jane was very much the outdoor girl, either riding, swimming or playing hockey. Domesticity didn't fit into her scheme of life and I couldn't really see her carrying out telephone duties for the rest of her days! We had a long discussion as to how to cope with this domineering lady. He suggested that to spread the load a bit we might ask Mary and Tom to dilute her presence. Before we headed homewards we decided on a technique for handling this wayward filly, and in a crisis we might, resort to Plan B.

On the eve of the ball we dropped in for a drink and drove off together. It was a formal affair so we tried to appear sophisticated in our dinner jackets. The ladies were very beautiful in evening dress, Moira in the coppery shot silk dress which I always admired. Jane, in an emerald, off the shoulder gown, which went so well with her deep red shoulder length tresses, had many heads turning. Tom dwarfed us all in his dinner jacket which accentuated his Nordic blond hair. Mary, dressed in a deep blue ball gown moulded to her slim figure was bubbling over with joy. Moira, arrayed in her ravishing 'Autumn Leaves' ball gown caught the tail end of our conversation and nearly let the cat out of the bag by asking Brian if Plan B was part of his strategy for building new kennels.

As the ladies departed to powder their noses, Brian said uneasily "Do you see what I mean, this is her hunting garb and I'm the fox. If I'm not careful it will be Tallyho and I'll be walking up the aisle!"

Don't worry too much Brian," quipped Tom with a wicked smile. "We shall flush her out of her lair!"

I could appreciate Jane's attraction at once. Fresh complexioned with green eyes, she had the broad shoulders of an accomplished swimmer and a dominating personality which created a commanding presence in the crowd. She readily laughed when Brian and I quipped about the people in the room, although I sensed that it was a bit forced and that there was a steely intent beneath the mirth. She and Mary chattered away about mutual acquaintances in the horse world although, as Mary said later, that her set were not always the most savoury.

We were all enjoying the evening, with the possible exception of Brian who had several severe coughing spasms in the smoky atmosphere, particularly after galloping around the room to the tune of the Gay Gordons. I felt that Jane became slightly irritated after each coughing bout and as I glimpsed at Brian I imagined that I saw a twinkle in his eye.

We were relaxing in the lounge when the pageboy arrived with a message that Ruth was on the telephone. This made me feel somewhat uneasy, as such interruptions during an evening out were generally an emergency, which meant an end to the night's frolics. Brian returned, smiling broadly. "You must excuse me for a wee moment. Old Amelia Quayle, a dear old lady well on in her eighties, is worried because her budgie Cuthbert has fallen off his perch. Cuthbert is also pretty ancient and I have been wondering lately which of them would fall off their perch first. Anyway, she is in love with me and wants to see me in my dinner jacket. I'll be back in a few minutes".

As he departed, Jane commented that it was a bit hard that an old lady's budgie should take precedence over an evening's pleasure. She had a lot to learn!

To make up for Brian's abscence Tom scooped Jane up in his arms and took her onto the floor to join in the Gay Gordons. He applied all his Young Farmers zest into the dance and Jane's feet were not on the floor for much of the time. She returned to the table looking quite exhausted and subdued. I had only been taking Moira on the floor for the less strenuous dances as she was feeling the effects of her pregnancy.

I felt it incumbent upon me to ask Jane to join in the Viennese Waltz, a most graceful dance when carried out with skill. All went well until the end when I slipped on a spilt drink which resulted in me lying flat on my back on the floor desperately clutching a voluptuous redhead to my chest. This brought great cheers from my friends as I escorted the visibly shaken lady back to our table.

Brian's visit actually took a while longer than anticipated, despite the fact that Amelia only lived a short distance away. On his return, Brian bent double and, red in the face with paroxysms of coughing. We sat him down with a glass of water to find that most of his problem was laughter.

Dear old Amelia had met him at the door and hurried him into the sitting room, only to find that Cuthbert had miraculously recovered and was sitting shakily, on his perch. "Oh! Mr Scanlon! I'm so sorry to have dragged you away from the ball. They are such jolly affairs with lots of laughter. I used to work at the Castle Mona and wait on at table before I met my Fred. Then it wasn't right for a respectable married woman to go out working, so I stayed at home and raised the children. I'm so glad that you could see Cuthbert. He's my only contact with my Fred since he died last year. He put so much work into that bird and taught him to say all sorts of words."

Brian had tentatively put his finger into the cage to see if Cuthbert was fit to perch on it. Cuthbert greeted him with an icy stare, as he knew about vets, leant forward, pecked Brian painfully on the thumb and very clearly said, "B----r off!", and returned to preening himself in front of his mirror.

Amelia a pillar of the chapel, was mortified and, as Brian made a tactical retreat, she was berating the poor bird and demanding to know where he had picked up that awful expression.

Jane didn't seem to join in our hilarity, possibly because she was no longer the centre of attention. We decided to head for home as Brian was feeling a bit below par. He really must feel better in the morning as he was entertaining Jane all weekend and needed to keep up his strength for the chase. Before heading homewards the Castle Mona staff, as was their custom, appeared bearing trays laden with mugs of steaming Bovril, either to ward off evil spirits or hangovers!

Several days had passed since the ball and Moira had even forgiven me for my behaviour at the dance. Lying on the floor of a ballroom clutching a lusty redhead to my chest was inclined to generate widespread speculation in the Manx gossip columns! We had not seen Brian during the weekend, so I arranged with Mary that we should be entertained by him before heading for home.

As I lay down to sleep, my mind drifted towards Brian's adventures during the weekend and the success of our plan to cope with the irrepressible Jane.

I thought that I would drop into town before heading home for the evening. I followed Mary's rather battered jallopy into town and we pulled in as we saw Brian's car parked outside the Woodburn Hotel, and could not resist the idea of a post mortem on his weekend's frolics.

Brian was standing at the bar with old George Kaighin and Gyp who had dropped in for their evening pint. "Oh Mr Carson and a young lady, lovely to see yer'. It's about time Gyp and I went home to look after Daisy. You have a good chat with Mr Scanlon."

Brian ordered another pint and said, "You can't wait to hear the news? You're a real old Manx skeet!"

"Come on Brian. Tell me how the weekend went before I have to hear the banns read in church, I asked Mary to call in with me to act as an independent witness. Anyway you may wish her to be a bridesmaid."

With a twinkle in his eye Brian said, "Well! Lady Jane was bouncing on Sunday morning after the dance, so I took her hacking across the hills to reduce her head of steam. This was followed by a hearty lunch and a brisk walk around Derbyhaven. Of course you can imagine that I lagged behind and coughed at great length. At this stage I suspect that she was having second thoughts about sharing her life with a semi-invalid."

The tale was now warming up so I felt it my duty to buy the next round." Well, come on. Did you have to resort to plan B?"

Brian was relishing the story and trying to string it out. "Of course time was getting short and desperate situations require drastic measures. You might almost call it my Swan Song. I sensed that we were nearing the stage when she was going to propose to me!

Anyway, I arranged for a romantic candlelit dinner at the Fort Anne Hotel. The situation was perfect, the food magnificent with a remarkable red wine to complement the main course. A charming young man, a beautiful woman slightly overwhelmed by the atmosphere and the wine.

After coffee in the lounge I suggested a moonlight stroll along the Marine Drive."

At this point he lapsed into a romantic reverie, rehearsed for my benefit. With a smile he chuckled quietly to himself. "It's like this Ned. All's fair in love and war and I had to resort to Plan B!

Of course the night air started me coughing more than ever as I walked along lost in thought. After a few minutes Jane was becoming somewhat concerned so I eventually stammered out. "Jane, my dear, I don't know how to tell you this as I wanted our last day together to be perfect. I had a phone call from the doctor yesterday to say that he is pretty sure that I have tuberculosis, possibly caught from cattle. This means a lengthy course of treatment, possibly in a clinic, and that I must avoid close contact with people. It will be lonely without you, but I feel that we should not meet until I am completely recovered in about three years time."

"She audibly gasped and moved away from me, even sat in the back of the car on the journey home. Farewell to the love of my life! As we discussed in Plan B, most hearty outdoor types are frightened of diseases!"

Mary gasped! "How could you deceive the lady so?"

61

"Quite easily", responded Brian smiling broadly. "It was a case of do or die really!"

Our mission accomplished - I drove home to Peel, to tell Moira the glad tidings.

One of the greatest joys of veterinary practice is the unexpected. I would wake up each morning with the tickly feeling, what will happen today? I never pursued situations but they seemed to lie in wait for my arrival.

One of my Round Table friends was David Humphreys, a busy young solicitor with a keen eye on climbing the ladder of success. It came as no surprise to us when he announced his forthcoming marriage to Fiona, a wealthy young lady from Chester, whom he had met on a rather hectic Round Table weekend. She was petite and vivacious with auburn hair and roguish green eyes, which twinkled with mischief. Most of us could not attend the wedding as it was midweek and a three day trip for impoverished newly weds was out of the question.

I didn't speak to Dave for several weeks until one morning he 'phoned me at seven a.m. "Could you help me out Ned? I have a business appointment in Douglas at 8 a.m. and Fiona has problems with Rufus, our Labrador. He's a bit of a clumsy clot and caught the tip of his tail in the door yesterday and every time he sees us he wags his tail with great enthusiasm and the walls and furniture are starting to get covered with blood spots. Would it be too much to ask you to call into Glen Vine and see him on your way to into Douglas?"

"My dear Dave, don't worry about it. If Fiona is at home to help me restrain the hooligan I'll call at eight o'clock. I realise that he is a bear of little brain so she will be a great asset."

I had no intention of taking Rufus to the surgery. He would be leaping all over me and the thought of my beloved car being covered with blood was too much. A quick breakfast, a fond farewell to Moira and I set off for Glen Vine, where the Humphreys had just bought a new house. Walking up the garden path I could see Rufus, through the glass door, prancing about at the thought of a visitor.

I rang the doorbell and it was several minutes before I saw an ephemeral figure floating down the stairs. The door opened and I was greeted by Fiona, looking gorgeous, clad in a diaphanous negligée and a seductive aura of bath oils, hanging onto the collar of the rumbustious Rufus.

I stared open mouthed at this delightful apparition as Fiona blushed and giggled. "Come in quickly Ned so that we can control this monster." Each time she screamed orders at him, Rufus looked suitably delighted at holding our attention and tried to leap all over us.

"I'm terribly sorry." continued Fiona contritely. "Dave didn't tell me that you would be here so early so I settled down to luxuriate in a nice warm bath."

"Right!" I replied, trying to get a grasp on reality and give the impression that it was an everyday matter to interview scantily dressed ladies.

"Where can we examine and restrain Rufus, preferably on a bench? Let's take him in here to the kitchen and we can put him on the formica covered table. It will clean up easily. As I lift him up, can you push his front leg away from you, lean over his head and I'll do the same at the rear end." With one great heave we lifted all seventy pounds of wriggling dog onto the table and lay across his body- Fiona coping with the slobbering end whilst I was flagellated by his bloody tail!

It was all becoming very personal as we both snuggled up close, restraining the dog, whilst I was being constantly assailed by clouds of bath oil and talc. Fiona sensed the situation and giggled coquettishly. I had a quick word with my maker, confirming my marriage vows and calling for urgent assistance before the ship sank with all hands. I wondered what Professor Kelly's advice would have been in my situation. 'Probably to make a careful diagnosis and consider all options'.

"Listen to me carefully, Fiona", I said. "Every time Rufus wags his tail the wound will break down so I shall arrange a shield over the area"

I leant down to open my case, which lay on the floor and single handedly extracted scissors, bandage, Elastoplast and one of Moira's curlers.

"I am going to clip off all the hair away for eight inches from the tip, dress the wound with ointment and cover with gauze and cotton wool as protection; apply Moira's hair roller as a protective cage and cover the lot with a layer of Elastoplast extending half way up the tail."

Each time that I turned to talk to her I was aware of those twinkling eyes watching me carefully and looking into mine, the clouds of perfume and I was sure she was edging along the dog's ribcage towards me. My mind was in turmoil as lurid thoughts of Arabian nights kept intruding on my silent appeals for help to my maker, when the now electric atmosphere was shattered by the strident, undoubtedly female voice coming through the serving hatch

"Stop it. You dirty old bugger!"- Armageddon! Whatever would Granny Carson, back in Ulster, have thought of such language!

There was a deafening silence, for what seemed like an hour. I almost let go of reality and clutched the edge of the table, Rufus fell onto the floor and continued his game and Fiona collapsed into a chair convulsed with laughter."

"Oh Ned! The timing was perfect. That's our Mynah bird, 'Jorrocks', who Dave has taught to say that in my voice! On top of that, you look delicious covered with bloody freckles."

"Thank the Lord!" I gasped. "I thought that it was your mother and I still don't believe your explanation! David could not imitate your dulcet tones so accurately." As I looked in the mirror with a sigh of relief I had a quick word with 'himself' for helping me out of a sticky corner.

"I think that I could now do with a wash to remove the blood spots, followed by a cup of tea to steady my nerves before surgery. Can you bring him into surgery in a week's time, when we shall have the manpower to handle him."

We had a complete Saturday to ourselves. The stress of a two man practice was easing since the arrival of Mary. We opted to push Donal into Peel and do some shopping, even though Moira was tiring more easily as her pregnancy progressed. It was a delight to spend time together without time being a limiting factor. Just to be able to call in with friends and chat at leisure was so relaxing. After talking to Ernest Cowley the chemist, I had to call in at the Post Office and then collect my copy of the 'Peel City Guardian'. It was always a challenge to read and try and conjure up the missing words as the print sometimes failed.

As we were walking through the square I commented to Moira that the new postwoman had just gone up Atholl Street and that there was something familiar about her which I could not fathom. A case of 'déja vu'! It was still niggling in my brain when we saw her walking along Michael Street, something familiar about her movement and body language. We'd met before!

"She delivered our post the other day!" said Moira, "I had a brief word with her, an attractive lady-well spoken! Indeed she asked if you were Ned Carson. I said yes and she replied that you had met before! Could she be one of your amours? Anyway let's head home for coffee as I'm tiring"

The following week we went walking along the beach at Peel and approached a couple who were beachcasting - probably for bass. As the lady turned round - a petite impish face set in a halo of blonde curls - I saw that this was our mystery post lady -Vera Sutherland! I rushed forward to greet her.

"Moira, meet Vera Sutherland, our mystery postwoman. I'm so glad to see you. Brian assigned me to track you down. What are you doing in Peel City?"

Vera greeted Moira. "I'm so glad to see you both together. It's very confusing, when one arrives in a new area, to connect people. By the way, I'm not Sutherland any more. Meet Tom Quirk, my husband. After a rather loveless relationship with Graham I met Tom, who drove the post van around the North. His wife, Julia died several years ago and he was trying to rear his daughter by himself. We found that we had much in common.

Graham was itching to return to Africa and I desperately wanted to start a family so we agreed to go our separate ways. I can't tell you how happy I am"

"We're delighted to see you in Peel. Where are you living? More importantly. Have you caught any bass?"

"The answer to your last question is no only a couple of 'flatties'. But if you look up on the front, there is a cottage with a shop front. That's headquarters which we share with Tom's mother. There's also room for me to run a cafe and keep an eye on the family 'cos the good news is that I'm expecting twins in about four months. Peel front should be a lovely safe spot to rear children! Our own little spot in heaven. Tom's mum also has the franchise for the ferry across the harbour so there's an extra job for you in the summer, Ned! Get a fisherman's hat on and you would fit in perfectly!"

"Congratulations twice! As you can see we are looking forward to an addition soon. It will be nice to have good neighbours and you ladies can enjoy baby chat."

The cross we have to bear in a caring profession is the client, who invariably calls on a Sunday or in the evenings. "I'm so sorry to ring you now but I thought that you would not be too busy!"

It had been a fairly hectic Sunday afternoon in January. I had watched the fog bank slowly creeping silently in from the western sea, enveloping Peel Castle and moving eastwards until it held the whole island in it's clammy embrace. Visibility was reduced to fifty yards, particularly across the hilltops, where black faced sheep seemed to suddenly appear, on the road from nowhere, confused and unsure where they were going, or from whence they had come. Silence was complete. Even the birds sat huddled on the dripping branches, glad of some shelter.

In conditions such as these myths are born, where shadows or figures come and go at the limits of vision. Tales which I had heard since childhood of mermaids, the Tarroo-Ushtey or Water bull and the Phynnoderee, a great hairy giant of a man, who helped out farmers by carrying out their field work in the dark of the night.

Gazing into the flickering flames of a warm fire with Moira during the evening meal, life was perfect. The sound of the telephone abruptly broke the silence. Lifting the receiver and anticipating problems I commenced, "Ned Carson here. Can I help you?"

"Oh Mr Carson!," shrilled the all too familiar tones of Dottie Willman-Jones. I grimaced and gave Moira the thumbs down!

"Can you come quickly. My lovely little Salome is in such pain, rolling in agony on the floor. My dinner guests will be so upset. Her little friend Mitzi is most concerned at her odd behaviour. She had a colic like this earlier this afternoon. Please come quickly," she continued with a sob in her voice. "I hope that she won't die!"

Rolling my eyes I sent a silent prayer upwards, "Why me?" I attempted to sound fascinated with

Salome's problems, whilst I rapidly shovelled in my sausage and mash and replied, "I'll be with you as soon as possible Mrs Willman-Jones. In the mean time leave her as quiet as you can. The fog is so thick out here that I can hardly see a car's length in front."

It took a good half hour to reach Douglas. En-route I ran through all the possible diagnoses on the plight of Salome, who was a young and skinny Siamese cat with cross-eyes and a distinct lack of academic achievement. Despite these drawbacks she was the beloved companion of Mitzi, the Cairn terrier, who regarded herself as the carer for an educationally subnormal cat. Driving through the grey night, my mind was running through the textbooks for a diagnosis. Was the kitten having fits because of roundworms or had she developed an abscess?

Pulling up outside her splendid house, known locally as "Dollyville", I saw that it was a blaze of lights, like Douglas promenade at high season. I managed to squeeze my sturdy little Morris 1000 in between a large Rover and the Jaguar, which I recognised as belonging to 'Puffin Billy' Bernstein the lawyer.

The irrepressible Dottie was in party mode once more! Entering the front door was akin to going into a chicken house at feeding time when the cackling reaches a crescendo.

Arthur, the ex-R.A.F. type was once more acting as major-domo for Dottie and rushed out to greet me. "Jolly good show that you managed to turn out tonight," he commenced exhuberantly. "Suppose that you've got to be ready to scramble at any time day and night. Wouldn't want your job old boy! Dear old Dottie is in a terrible tiz about her scrawny old moggie."

As he showed me into the dining room, I recognised most of the party. Billy and Audrey Bernstein were talking to Dottie whilst on the far side was the tall stooped figure of Charles De Vere Pullen with his wife Daphne, engrossed in conversation with a young couple, who were strangers. Dottie introduced them as David and Agnes Blatchford. He was the newly-arrived curate in Onchan. He had been a captain in the Devonshire Light Infantry before entering the church to fight the good fight on other fronts.

The other couple I remembered as the Lieut. Governor of the Isle of Man, Sir Ainsley and Lady Relph. They had all quenched their thirst and were in expansive mood. As ever Billy was holding court, engulfed in a fragrant Havana aura.

Dottie was resplendent in a large ladies version of that "little black dress", that made her appear absolutely enormous. It was decorated with intricate sequined patterns which sparkled and shone like the clearance lights on a heavy goods vehicle.

Dottie continued. "Oh Mr Carson, I do apologise for dragging you out on such a miserable night. You must be so busy with Mr Scanlon being indisposed. I do hope that his cold is better. Daphne is so concerned that he may not be fit for the Pony Club event next weekend. However, I am very worried about Salome who has now retired to her bed in the corner. Poor soul, she must be so exhausted by now."

She mine swept across the room to Salome's basket, pausing only to pick up a glass of claret, and place it in my hand. "I do hope that I've not dragged you out on a wild goose chase as she appears to have settled now!"

I examined Salome, who had been decorated with a blue ribbon, as part of the party spirit. With the eager assistance of Mitzi, who appeared to be suffering from "potato crisp bloat", I chatted with the patient and looked her over carefully.

Salome was delighted to have my undivided attention and purred and rubbed against me in a most enthusiastic manner. I could find very little amiss with her from a clinical viewpoint but as I turned to speak to Dottie she reacted most strangely. She writhed on her back on the floor emitting deep throated yowls like a soul in torment. All eyes turned upon her as she then lay on her belly on the carpet and stuck her back end in the air whilst producing the most agonising cries.

Dottie knelt down beside her and crooned. "Oh my little lamb, tell mumsy, is your tum-tum really sore? Mr Carson, what can we do for her?"

"Don't be so daft, Dottie," barked Daphne in her inimitable parade ground manner. "The cat's a raving nymphomaniac. Sexy little trollop. My young filly is just the same when she's horseing. She reminds me of a stable girl we used to have. Every time my son appeared she went all girly and wiggly."

"Oh no," uttered Dottie in disbelief immediately connecting "horseing" with "whorseing"

I could see that the audience was all agog. Even the curate was heard to comment. "There must be a basis for a sermon somewhere in this! How about 'Lust Must' "

I replied with some deliberation. "Mrs Willman-Jones shall we discuss this in the hallway"

"Of course not, Mr Carson. After your unerring diagnosis at Christmas I've told all my friends how clever you are."

"Well!" I said hesitantly and somewhat flattered. "It is a slightly sensitive subject. As Mrs Pullen said, she is in season. Siamese cats behave like this when they are in season. She is acting like a sex kitten and you will be serenaded for the next few days. All the tomcats in the neighbourhood will be dropping in for afternoon tea unless you can get her off to a cattery."

Trying hard to maintain a serious mien, I continued, "Come to think of it, I have never seen a litter of Manx Siamese! Perhaps you could start a new fashion. Once this all settles down I feel that you should have her spayed".

Dottie blushed deeply, the Lieutenant Governor stared steadfastly into his brandy, possibly considering his past encounters and the Blatchfords giggled uncontrollably at the weakness of the flesh. Billy was chortling with laughter and desperately clinging on to his seat. "Good Lord Dottie. The cat's a harlot. It just isn't seemly. What will the neighbours say? A feline bordello - no less! I'll bet that they cannot better this tale in the Inns of Court!"

"Oh! Mr Carson. You are so kind. Here I am making a fool of myself and dragging you out on a fool's errand. How can I make amends?"

"We could consider this as 'C'est La Vie', I responded. For your sake I think the best remedy would be to give me a call as soon as she gives up the Mata Hari act and we can have her deflowered. I must leave you now as I am on call by myself until Brian is quite recovered."

On my way back home I pondered on the manner in which people were losing their sense of values about animals due to the population drift away from the land. Many people were beginning to look upon pets as objects to satisfy their own emotional needs instead of companion animals. It was a developing problem. Only that week I had been presented with a poodle for treatment and the owner had painted it's toenails to match her own. This was a sop to her own vanity with no thought about the dog and poor little "Pixie" became a fashion accessory. I thought sadly that from the animal's viewpoint it was a case of "Lord preserve us from our friends."

If they could only come with me and see sheep pigs and poultry being slaughtered, compassionately on the farm, they might view life more realistically. Farmers over the centuries had killed their own animals or had a local slaughterman in to prepare the animals for home consumption. As they had associated with these beasts during their lives the animals were slaughtered with great compassion.

As I grew up in the war years many people possessed sheepskin rugs, ostensibly from animals which had died, but really as an offshoot of the black market in meat.

13

Fenella and her brother Ernie Quane lived happily enough at The Hope, St Johns. Their parents had farmed there before them but as they became more infirm much of Fenella's time was involved in caring for the ageing couple. At sixty five years old her mother went to bed with an attack of the 'bronicals' and Fenella looked after her day and night. This suited the old lady admirably so she reclined in her bed for the rest of her days with the exception of Christmas day and the Sabbath, when she would struggle out to chapel. This put all the farm work onto Fenella and her father as such menial jobs were beneath her brother.

Ernest was a man of stature with a great interest in the political goings on in the Island so he eventually ended up as the Member of the House of Keys for the electoral area or sheading as suited a man of importance. His tenure in government did not last too long, so he reverted to the post of Coroner for Glen Maye, which is akin

79

to taking the Chiltern Hundreds. Most evenings he could be found talking politics in the Market Inn, following in the footsteps of famous people like his predecessor, Ebenezer Quirk, and hurling insults across the bar at Danny Horne. At the end of the evening they would ride off together, still arguing and singing unseemly songs. Ernest's path would lead him off to Patrick, in the direction of Glenmaye where he had a batchelor house perched high on the clifftops.

Despite being a man of mature years he would often contact Moira and myself at the time of the Springtides for an afternoon's 'crabbing' at low tide. We would set off across the seaweed covered rocks with our crabbing hooks and a hessian sack where we started at the water's edge. Soon we were probing under the rocks, winkling out the large and active crabs and dropping them into the sack before taking them home The skill was to avoid those nutcracker claws by grabbing the crab firmly by the back of the shell. We were amazed at the ease with which Ernest skipped across the weed covered rocks in his hobnailed boots whilst we slipped and slithered behind him.

Fenella didn't have many cattle but she was blessed with plenty of grass as a result of which her stock flourished and grew fat. Unfortunately, she always forgot to call us to castrate her single suckled calves, until they were yearlings. This caused problems for the poor unfortunate vet who had to carry out the procedure, as even before the operation the yearlings behaved like spoilt children and leapt about kicking and bawling when they were restrained!

We felt that it was unfair to send Mary castrating this motley crew on her own, so I was volunteered to add the manpower as most of the local farm workers were helping with the harvest. Mary offered, against my better judgement, to drive us in her rickety old Hillman.

Fenella was waiting in the yard as the car wheezed to a standstill. "Follow me!" she commanded. "We drove these little darlin's into the loosebox by themselves lest their mammies might get overexcited and 'ave a go at yer! Fortunately, Johnny Kinrade, the postman has offered to help Ernest with the holding. They're up in the 'hackett' collectin' a few bales of straw to cover up the mess as we knaw that you vetinries like it all tidy!"

I had heard about Johnny, who was one of Fenella's admirers. She was a very big, handsome woman, who seemed to have spent many years repulsing those suitors who did not come up to her standards. He was a small wiry man, seeming to counterbalance Fenella who swept her statuesque figure around like a schooner in full sail!

As I opened the loosebox door there was a crashing and banging as four wild-eyed yearlings tried to climb the walls or escape into the feedrack. At that moment Ernest and Johnny appeared, each toting a couple of bales of straw. We let them inside where they cut open the bails and scattered straw across the floor amidst the flailing feet. All this time the two border collies lay on duty, nose between fore feet watching the door lest any calves might try to slip past.

Once the dust had settled we entered quietly whilst the yearlings rewstarted their wall-of-death performance around the loosebox. I had brought a rope in with me and dropped it over a calf's neck. My victim came to an abrupt halt as I slipped the rope through a ring in the wall and held him firmly against the stonework. He bawled and struggled but the rest of the team joined me to restrain him. With one final leap he kicked straight out behind and Johnny dropped, pole-axed clutching his crutch and groaning. This was not a good move on his part as the next moment an enraged Fenella, revealing her heart's passion, grabbed the calf's head in a vice-like grip shouting "You little bugger. You don't kick my Johnny like that! Cut his balls off miss!" Mary appeared from nowhere, scalpel in hand, and in a trice the calf was deflowered!

Johnny staggered to his feet and like a feisty little terrier, pushing Fenella aside, grabbed the next surprised calf before he had time to complain. Having acquired the technique, the team made short work of the remaining calves before turning them out on the pasture to be reunited with their worried mums.

Fenella called us into the kitchen for tea and home-made rock buns. "Thanks for doing that job Miss Sutherland. I must apologise as I've seen the error of my ways. It's easy enough to put off these operations until the bullocks are too big and hard to handle. Next time they'll be done under two months old and we might think of this new dehorning technique as well."

Heading back to the car I noticed that Mary was limping quite badly. "What's the problem?" I said. "Did you get kicked as well?"

"Something similar!" was her response." One of the little darlin's slid it's foot down my shin and then onto my instep. Not very nice!" At that point she removed her wellington with difficulty and already the limb was inflamed and swollen.

"Fear not. Dr Carson will sort you out when we get back to the surgery. If we dress that with tincture of Arnica and Wych Hazel your problems will melt away. It's all part of the magic of homoeopathy. Much against my better judgement I insist on driving you home in Chitty Chitty Bangbang as you won't be able to drive safely!"

With great self control she turned round to face me with eyes flashing. "Thank you Dr Carson! I accept your offer as I am in great pain. When I am recovered you could be in danger of assault! In the meantime take me home for treatment."

"Climb aboard, madam. I'm glad that you are converted to homoeopathy. Allow me a minute's silence whilst I pray for a safe journey home!"

The sturdy little Hillman started off wheezing and groaning and showing distinct evidence of a limp as we sped down the road.

Passing The Hawthorn Inn and St Trinian's church I suggested that Mary ask the fairies, who lived in the church, to look after us on the journey. A stony silence greeted my suggestion. Evidently, she was an unbeliever!

Bumpety-bump we went through Glenvine, past Glenlough Farm to the long descent into Union Mills. We were doing a rattling good fifty miles an hour when I felt the car relax slightly and glanced out of the driver's side window.

"Mary!" I said quietly but urgently. "Remain completely calm and don't shift in your seat. I can't say what is going to happen but on our right-hand side is the rear wheel, overtaking us down the hill! If we lean to the left and gently slow down I shall attempt to pull into the verge."

Like a couple of motorcyclists we moved our weight to the left. Mary was almost rigid with anticipation as we slowly came to a halt and our eyes met in absolute relief. Quietly she put her hand on my knee and said, "Ned! Next time I'll have a word with those fairies as I pass!"

I stepped out, retrieved the wandering wheel from the opposite hedge and walked down to the nearby cottage to phone for help. It was a delight to hear Alan's voice at the other end chortling with delight. "I knew it! You two aren't fit to be sent out together. Stay there and I'll come out and pick you up. Summat tells me that the little car has reached the end of it's days and should be put down! Happen Mary might be safer wi' a horse and cart!"

Of course the story was across the Island like wildfire and the chat in the Jolly Farmer was about the effect that the young lady vet was having on Ned's driving. Only bribery in the shape of a pint helped to subdue the rumours.

In a small holding, beside Gleneedle, up behind Foxdale pub, Danny Horne lived happily with his family, which included two Tamworth sows, a Large White boar called Eustace and numerous sheep and ponies and a long suffering wife.

As an ex Motor Torpedo Boat skipper he had commanded his crew through the D-Day landings. As an ex publican and larger-than life eccentric, he was a formidable figure of a man. At twenty stone, black-bearded with a pony tail he had used this image and his personality as mine host to draw in the crowds. His deep sonorous voice dominated the room and led to his nickname of "Fog Horne". He even went to the length of serving in the bar with Pedro, his African parrot, on his shoulder. Every time he rang the bell at closing time Pedro would scream out "Time you idle lubbers, P....off home".

Pedro's achille's heel, as with so many of us, was the opposite sex. He was wont to fall passionately in love with all feathered creatures until one day he was found to be making amorous advances to a feather boa belonging to a guest at a wedding reception. Unfortunately, the lady was still attached to the boa and as it was being wrested from Pedro's clutches his language would have done credit to a fishwife. "You're a lovely bit of crumpet, you silly old strumpet!" After this little episode he was banned from public functions!

Danny first achieved notoriety throughout the island when he took "Flower", his Aberdeen Angus heifer to the fat stock sale in the Ramsey Cattle Market. Flower had been kept indoors for several months to fatten her up.

A few days before the sale I had a rather worried Danny on the phone- "Sorry to bother you Ned, but Flower is due to go to market and is a bit constipated after eating too much dry roughage. Can you let me have something for her that won't affect the meat?"

"Yes," I replied, "Try drenching her with a pint and a half of treacle."

"Great idea! Thanks!"

"Actually, I won't charge you for that advice but you may feel indebted when we meet at the Market Inn!"

Always generous to fault, Danny drenched her with three pints of the tasty laxative, to make sure of the job.

In Ramsey mart, a murmuring crowd of farmers, each with an eye for a bargain, leaned on the rail surrounding the ring as Flower was guided in by a drover whilst the auctioneer wound up the bidding. She was fairly docile so the attendant almost had to push this sleek butterball around the ring. Suddenly, she stopped, took in a deep breath and coughed, a deep chesty cough. At the other end the unfortunate drover saw her tail rise, tried to move too late, and found himself instantaneously clad from head to toe in a mixture containing three pints of treacle laced with cow dung.

Time stood still and silence gripped the crowd around the arena before roars of applause and laughter broke out as the unfortunate victim tried to clear his mouth and nostrils of the gooey coating. It was probably a good thing that he didn't die as there would have been no acceptable entry on his death certificate. Struggling to regain his composure, Raymond Kewin, the auctioneer shouted across the ring, "What do you call this beast, Danny."

The immediate retort was "Treacle Bum, Raymond!" which delighted the audience further.

Of course, bad news travels fast in the island and by the time Danny arrived in the pub that evening he was greeted by a chorus of "Danny, Danny, treacle bum!"

Eustace, the large white boar had been adopted by Danny as company for his pet lambs. Passing motorists were extremely surprised to see this larger than life figure, with a parrot on his shoulder, striding down the road with two half-grown lambs and a young boar trotting along behind.

Eustace went through life firmly believing that he was a dog as he had grown up and slept with Jake the labrador since they were both toddlers. They scampered across the fields together, with Danny who taught them both to retrieve sticks and balls. Pedro would sit on Danny's shoulder calling the dog back with a shrill whistle or shouting "Here little piglet. Bring the stick back to daddy."

As Eustace grew older there came the time to 'put aside childish things' and apart from his adolescent vices, concentrate on the more mature aspects of life such as propagation of the species. These duties he carried out with great zest and efficiency.

His greatest vice, however, was an addiction to alcohol. Whether this yobbish behaviour developed from the addition of a food supplement to his trough in the form of brewer's grains or from sharing his owners love of home brewing, is fortunately, lost in the mists of time. Danny could be found leaning on the garden wall imbibing his home made-beer from a quart jug whilst Eustace leant over the wall beside him and was fed his beer from a pint glass with a handle. Then they would both retire to sleep it off in the sun. He had to take 'several-drying out' sessions as an inebriated boar is inclined to fall off his target at mating time.

Another great joy of Danny's life was Xerxes, his sturdy little Welsh cob who had to be sturdy to carry his weight. In many ways he was Danny's saviour and transport to the Market Inn in St Johns. Driving the car back home from St Johns was inclined to be hazardous after a convivial evening with friends, as the almost straight road became somewhat circuitous.

The idea came home to Danny one evening as he studied the old photographs in the pub and found one of his illustrious predecessor, Ebenezer Quirk. From that night onwards Xerxes would be saddled up and ridden to the pub. As he tied the long suffering animal to the pump in the yard of the hostelry he announced himself with an impressive rendition of "Oh! For the wings of a dove!" In a rich bass baritone.

Returning home later in the evening he clung on tight and relied on Xerxes unerring homing instinct whilst the neighbours were serenaded with "Oh What a beautiful morning". However, passing years and Danny were beginning to weigh heavily upon Xerxes constitution and he found that the uphill gradient to Foxdale became increasingly difficult to negotiate.

It had been a relaxing evening off duty and Moira and I had walked over the headland, with dog and cat in close attendance, stalking each other through the long grass. After supper we sat down to watch the sun dropping over the horizon, leaving a golden trail, "St Patrick's Pathway" leading towards the silhouette of the Mourne Mountains.

Shortly after we retired to bed at half past eleven the 'phone shrilled and my dreams were rudely interrupted.

"Mr Carson, Peel Police here. Sorry to interrupt your slumbers but we have a problem at Foxdale near to the pub. A Mr Danny Horne has fallen off his horse on the main road. He is quite shaken up and the horse doesn't look very happy either. Can you have a sight at him in case it's serious? I've phoned the doctor, and he's on his way!"

I struggled into my clothes and out the front door. It was a beautiful, balmy night. The garden was aglow with the light of a full moon and the air sweet with the night-scented stock. In the distance an owl called, the gentle hoo-hoo breaking the silence. It was a pleasure to be out on such a night with the moonlit road stretching out before me.

As I drove up through Foxdale I could see a group of people at the roadside and P.C. Jack Careen waved me down with his flashlight. Danny, like a stranded whale, was huddled under the hedge moaning and grunting whilst the doctor examined him. Xerxes was standing beside him, head down and trembling in some distress. Superficially, apart from a couple of lacerated knees he looked all right. His pulse was bounding and he was breathing heavily, undoubtedly shocked by the accident. As I listened to his chest there was a regular hissing sound denoting a leaking heart valve!

Although slightly worse for wear Danny was able to give us a description of the incident.

"Oh Ned!" he said in a choked voice. "I've pushed my old friend too far. We were walking steadily up the hill, although he did seem a bit slow, when he staggered and fell down in the road, dumping me in the process. Lucky that I'm well padded or it could have been worse. What came over the old boy?"

"Well Danny, you told me a while ago that he was getting a bit long in the tooth. Tonight his age caught up with him. He's got a dodgy valve in his heart which could not cope with the hill so he ran out of oxygen and collapsed. He's retired as from tonight No more riding! I'll treat him tonight and call in to see him in the morning. If we speak to the folks in the pub he can stay in their stable tonight, well rugged up and with a warm bran mash. You have both had a lucky escape!"

Tears were streaming down Danny's face, and getting lost like so many little dewdrops in his beard, at the possible thought of losing his friend. "I hope he's not going to die, Ned. I should never forgive myself!"

When I called in to the pub next morning Xerxes was lapping up the attention of Danny and his five children, who were fussing over him with carrots and apples galore. Mickey, the youngest boy, a cheeky faced little blond with big "innocent" blue eyes, said with great concern, "He's not going to die is he, Mr Carson. We'll have no one to play with except Biddy the mare."

"I hope not, Mickey," I replied, "He's officially retired now. No more jumping him bareback in the paddock. Take Biddy across the jumps. She could do with losing some weight! Maybe Xerxes can give her some tips and she can take father down into the village from now on".

93

One evening Brian casually asked me if I would do a Saturday duty to help him out.

"Certainly," I responded. "Could I be so bold as to inquire where you are off to this weekend? Not another of your mysterious and seductive women? I do have a duty of care and concern for your welfare!"

There was a short pause, whilst he considered his reply. "No Ned! You Manx skeet! Always watching other people's business. Nothing so clandestine. Mary is hoping to ride Jade at the Southern show this year as her own pony is a bit long in the tooth. I suggested that we went off to the paddock this weekend and organised some jumps for her. You can come and give us a hand if you're not busy!"

"I'd be delighted." I replied. "I have passed my apprenticeship in erecting jumps and I should enjoy helping you both. Mary deserves a bit of a break as we have worked her extremely hard this year. Mind you, the stables could do with a bit of tidying before you lure another unsuspecting female into your lair. It's fortunate that horses don't talk of their experiences!" I quickly slipped out of the door before he thought out an appropriate response.

When Saturday morning arrived, Brian had already done an early morning call, so I took the first consultations. The waiting room was fairly empty except for a young mother, Rachel Carter, sitting patiently with her daughter and two little boys about three and five years old. I had seen families like this before in the public library and should have been on my guard. Mum traipses along the shelves examining the books to take home, whilst the children rush around the place shouting and arguing or, alternatively are very quiet while they pull books out of the shelves, scattering them on the floor.

Her children, Peter, Paul and Jane were bright-eyed with Nordic good looks. Their big blue eyes and dimples made one think of cherubs. Unfortunately, I overlooked the impish smile that flickered across Peter's face. The boredom factor is pronounced in bright children and, as soon as they entered the children deployed in several directions. Paul was peering into the wastepaper bin, Peter had the top off my treasured instrument tray, full of surgical spirit, and Jane had slipped out of the door leading into the house. This was a new world full of excitement and just waiting to be explored!

Rachel Carter, their mum, had brought in the family labradors, Flopsy and Rob, for vaccination. They were both in excellent fettle and Flopsy, the bitch, greeted me with great enthusiasm, almost climbing onto the table.

Rob, the dog was less forthcoming. His body language, as he entered the door, indicated his masculinity when he presented his body side on to me with hair on his back raised. He rumbled a deep warning, as I vaccinated him and Rachel held his head firmly. If I had made a mistake I might have been bitten! His duty was to look after Flopsy and the children, and woe betide anyone who interfered with his charges.

I glanced around to see the contents of the waste bin tipped on the floor. Peter was squirting spirit at the dogs with one of my precious glass syringes and Jane was being firmly but gently back into the consulting room by Ruth.

"I found this little stray on the upstairs landing, Mr Carson, sliding down the bannisters, indeed! It was only by the grace of God that she didn't fall onto the tiled floor and break her head open." There was a flicker behind the steel rimmed spectacles as she looked at Rachel and continued. "As it appeared to be a stray I thought that we might send her off to the dog's home!

Rachel rushed over and clung ever so tightly to her mother's skirt!

As they were leaving I smiled at Rachel and looked sternly at the children. "It's been nice to see you but remember that you must behave next time or I shan't ask you again!"

Peter, wide-eyed and innocent regarded me solemnly. "We're sorry if we caused any trouble Mr Carson, but everything is very interesting. Must the dogs behave as well?"

Completely beguiled by this naive approach I responded. "Yes of course, Peter. I'm sure that the dogs will behave very well."

Peter glanced at Paul and Jane, holding on to their mother and trying not to giggle. He looked straight at me, with the ghost of a smile on his face.

"Well in that case Mr Carson, you won't want to see Rob again, 'cos he's just pee'd over your shoe!"

At this stage, Rachel could restrain herself no longer, blushing deeply and scolding her chuckling family as she escorted them out of the room. Rob strutted out beside his charges - well satisfied with his morning's work. Later that morning a lovely box of chocolates arrived, with an apology from Rob.

Before rushing off to the stables, I had invited Mary in to check Fiona's idiot labrador Rufus so that we could compare techniques! I heard them arrive as there was a crashing in the waiting room. A few minutes later he rushed in with Fiona in full pursuit. The three of us laid him out on the examination table as I removed his tail dressing. I avoided eye contact with Fiona as she was in full bloom.

The tail had healed perfectly and I applied a light dressing before putting him on the floor. With a wicked gleam in her eyes, Fiona flung her arms around my neck and kissed me roundly before disappearing out the door. Smirking quietly, Mary quoted Val Callin and asked if Moira knew that I was carrying on with such an attractive woman, and perhaps, I should ask the fairies to look after me.

After surgery I called out to the stables to help with the jumps. Several had already been erected and Brian stood by supervising the action and commenting on progress. As I watched from a distance a thought stirred in my mind that he was using the same unconscious body language that came instinctively to him in the presence of the opposite sex. I could almost see the pheromones in the air as he worked his magic.

Alas. it fell on deaf ears as Mary was completely involved with controlling Jade around the jumps. The little mare responded to discipline of a confident rider and gave of her best. Eventually Mary was content with her performance and took her around the field a couple of times at full gallop. As they returned she jumped off and gave Jade a slap to show their mutual pleasure.

"She's ideal Brian, and very responsive to rein and heels. I'm sure that we'll be as one by the time the show comes round. Can I have a session with her again tomorrow, if you're not busy?"

"Don't worry", responded Brian in great delight. "Ned's on call tomorrow so we can make a day of it with maybe a ride over the hill and supper back at the house later!"

Sensing that I was surplus to requirements, I commented, "I'll take a bag of manure from the dung heap Brian and if all is quiet I'll present it to Moira to keep her roses blooming. Enjoy your weekend"

When I arrived home I remarked to Moira that Brian was in full bloom and she retorted, "It's only to be expected. He's a very attractive man. If I wasn't heavily pregnant, I might chase him myself"!

It transpired that Brian became more and more involved with show jumping during his weekends off duty. He was groom, companion and tutor for Mary during the run-up to the show and gymkhana season. Mary even went home to collect her beloved 'Minstrel' from Yorkshire as she hoped to compete regularly with her, and not always have to rely on borrowing Jade from Brian. As it turned out he was only too willing to loan Jade as well, so Mary had two mounts for competition.

He had a spring in his step which once more reminded me that life was good for him. I casually mentioned to Moira one evening that he was in lady killing mode and I suspected that Mary could well be the object of his affections.

One bright summer day there was a call from Rachel Carter requesting a visit to see Flopsy, who was not very well and appeared to have a lump on her tummy. It was fairly quiet, so I suggested that Mary came with me to meet this delightful, if somewhat naughty family. As soon as I rang the doorbell Rachel appeared looking wonderfully relaxed. "Oh! Mr Carson, We're so glad that you could come. It isn't very serious as Flopsy is always developing false pregnancies. Proffering her hand she continued, "I presume that you are Mary Sutherland. We have heard such glowing reports about you. My husband, Ben is supervising the children in the garden, we've just been taking photos. Do come through as I'm making tea.

We walked out through the french windows and found a game in full swing. We were greeted by a scene of domestic bliss. Ben was relaxing on a swing seat in the caressing warmth of the sun, keeping. an eye on the children's antics. "Have a seat" he said, "This has to be a day to remember!" Flopsy was stretched out on the lawn being tended by Jane. We could see at a distance that she hqad an extremely well-developed 'false pregnancy'.

Her breast was so enlarged that milk was flowing onto the grass. Jane was in attendance, squeezing milk into a teaspoon.

On the other side of the lawn Paul was solemnly pushing the doll's pram up and down. In the pram, tucked up under the blankets and wearing a bonnet, was 'Tiger' the cat, relishing all the attention.

Peter would collect a teaspoonful of milk from Jane, walk across to the pram and Tiger obligingly lapped it up, whilst being told that this medicine was good for him. Even Rob was too stunned by the warmth to welcome us.

After Rachel arrived with the tea we just sat and enjoyed the scene and chatted until eventually 'Tiger' became fed up with the attention, and a full bladder, and escaped into the bushes. It had been such an enjoyable episode that we had to drag ourselves away and promised to leave out tablets to dry up Flopsy's milk.

As we drove away Mary chuckled a comment, "That is one of the bonuses of practice. Why didn't I bring a camera? That was such a natural education for the children. It's a pity that city children couldn't see this enacted!"

As a teenager, I recalled seeing Billy Bates fishing off Douglas pier. He was a dirty, snotty-nosed little kid, whose clothes were always unkempt and ragged. He had not been dealt a straight hand of cards and was destined to exist at the bottom of the heap. He could be regarded as pretty nondescript until his big blue eyes would peer from beneath a mass of fair curly hair and an angelic smile would spread across his grimy features. "Hello mister! 'Ave yer caught any yet?"

Then an animated discussion on the fishing would ensue, and after much discussion and cajoling on his part, he would head off with all his catch and any surplus that any one else offered. I learnt later that much of this load of fish would be sold to friends on the way home and the remainder presented triumphantly to his mother to supplement the family's meagre ration.

As he was the eldest of a family of two boys and two girls, he took it upon himself to be a breadwinner and support his mother, who worked all hours taking in washing from other people's houses. Elsie, his mother, was a scrawny, unkempt woman, who had lost any looks she possessed maintaining her brood, whilst Frank, her husband drank his way through any money that she made. For years it had been a running battle trying to find new hiding places for money, which he eventually managed to ferret out.

Arriving back drunk after a night at the Market Inn, he would demand money and beat her mercilessly in front of the terrified children. By the time Billy was fourteen years old, he started answering Frank back and trying to defend his mother. This ended with him getting several beatings from his father which culminated in him being taken off to Noble's hospital with a broken arm. Eventually, in the middle of a stand up fracas between Elsie and Frank, he became so distraught that he dealt Frank a knock out blow with a heavy frying pan.

When Frank recovered consciousness next morning in Noble's Hospital, he fortunately had no recollection of the incident. Elsie sent Billy off for his own safety, to live with her sister, Joy, who ran a boarding house in Allan Street. Joy and husband Peter also ran a chip shop on Bucks Road and in no time Billy was in the shop helping to serve at table, dispensing Vimto to discerning customers and generally making himself useful.

All the time he was thinking of his mum and anything left over after closing time was wrapped up in newspaper and taken down to the family in Lord street flats, for supper. Shortly after Billy left home Frank was out on one of his drinking sprees and fell over the edge of the harbour at full tide. It was dark at the time, and the unfortunate Frank had never learned to swim, so his body was found next morning tangled in the moorings.

Through his contacts in the fishing industry Billy got a job, when he reached fifteen years old, in the Board of Agriculture checking on fish landings. His aptitude for the work and hard work eventually saw him promoted to foreman, which helped his mother's finances.

At this stage fate took a hand when he joined the Young Farmers Club and he became more involved in agriculture in the shape of Kathy Cowin, a farmer's daughter from The Garth. It was not a large farming enterprise, involving 15 dairy cows and 100 sheep.

Kathy used to invite Billy up to the farm for weekends to help out on the farm as her father was incapacitated with Parkinson's disease and mother had arthritis. Although Kathy was a very able young lady, she found that looking after the farm by herself was very hard work, particularly as she also helped out in the Crosby Post Office during the day.

Billy took to farming as if he had been born to it, and spent every spare hour helping with the stock. Of course Kathy's company was part of the honey trap and it wasn't long before they were walking up the aisle together. He still had a mop of fair curly locks and a wicked twinkle in those blue eyes but his every wish was to serve his young wife. When I looked back at his early days I could only be happy for them both.

Billy was an enterprising young man and it didn't take him long to persuade his new family to invest in pigs, which were a very profitable enterprise on a small farm. They resurrected the old calf shed and were soon working away building a new piggery, enough to hold half a dozen sows with outside pens for feeding and watering. The Landrace pig was the up and coming breed at the time on account of their temperament and food conversion rate. Billy had spent some time at Matt Munslow's piggery and decided that Large Whites were too agressive for his young bride. He also learned not to follow Matt's chaotic management system. Indeed, it didn't take many years before he and Kathy moved into a larger farm.

It was a beautiful spring day with low clouds scudding hurriedly across a bright blue sky. One minute we were enjoying the warmth of the sun on our backs and, within five minutes, scuttling for shelter away from the short heavy showers. To me this is always an exciting time as nature repeats it's cycle once again. There were stirrings of renewal in the land and one could almost hear the plants growing in the soil.

TheCuckoo

The Cuckoo comes in April
She sings her song in May
She changes her tune
In the month of June
In July she flies away

anon

I had already seen a couple of cuckoos and it wouldn't be long before those long summer days arrived, when I could lie back on the headlands just listening to the rapturous song of the skylark, as he climbed into the heavens. I have always been fascinated by the manner in which they disappear from view and yet the power of his liquid song continues unabated.

Brian had decided that it would be good for me to go and see Julie Jones in Port Erin. It was the junior colleague's privilege to confront the lady. She was a fluffy-haired blonde, very charming, but completely scatty. She had run a bric-a-brac shop in the village since her husband had fled to Australia, unable to cope with her lack of wit or any aspect of organisation in her life. Putting two logical thoughts together was a major operation for her. She had given up driving cars, as they all seemed to have a mind of their own and drift into the hedge at the slightest provocation.

Her vanity prevented her from wearing spectacles which would probably have solved her problem.

Her situation as a single, attractive lady created its own problems. Not only did she attract the male visitors but she also had a permanent clientele to carry her through the lean winter months. Invariably, she appeared at island festivities with a man in tow much to the discomfit of the native Methodist population. After all, a working girl has to earn a living somehow! Her claim to fame in the island was an article in a newspaper, entitled 'Love's Labours Lost', to the effect that the early morning peace of the village had been disturbed by the screams of anger from a local lady, absolutely nude, seen pursuing a cyclist clad in shorts along Station Road.

With these thoughts in mind and a few words with my Maker, I tentatively rang the front door bell. She greeted me effusively. "Oh! Mr Carson. I'm so glad you've come. You wouldn't believe the problems that I've had with these cats of mine. I love them dearly but they are driving me crazy! I was given these two beautiful Siamese kittens, Samson and Delilah. I still don't know whether they are boys or girls. They are so loveable but ever so naughty. Do come into the sitting room and see the mess that they have made."

The sitting room smelled quite strongly of cats even though I had not expected it to be pristine with Julie's reputation. As we walked into the room the cats were having a wonderful time chasing each other crazily about the room. It was a staggering sight of chaos as they raced over the furniture and swung on the curtains with gay abandon. The settee was threadbare, the curtains torn and big strips of paper hung off the walls.

As I sat down on the settee Julie joined me-close and comfortable. As she talked, her hands waved about and I spent my time dodging and weaving like a boxer. I was afraid that she was going to grasp me in a fierce embrace, so I stood up at a safe distance and listened.

"Look!" cried Julie in exasperation. "They have knocked over all my ornaments on the window sill and ripped the furniture. What can I do? I read somewhere that they operate and remove their claws in America. I'm at work all day, and I can't just keep an eye on them."

I quietly blessed Brian for suggesting that I came on this call as I tried to assemble my thoughts in some sort of order.

"Now let's look at it logically Mrs Jones. You have two very lively young cats, who are left indoors all day without supervision. You have supplied them with a litter tray, which they use regularly. If you had two young children in their place, they would probably get out of hand just as much. I would suggest that you make a run in the shed for them during the day, fitted out with a pole covered with carpet to exercise their claws and branches to climb on. Hang string from the ceiling with little paper bows on and leave a couple of Ping-Pong balls on the floor to play with. By the time you come home in the evening they will be pretty tired, but your house will still be in one piece."

"Thank you so much for your advice. I do hope that they will be happy in the shed by themselves!"

"Yes," I continued, somewhat exhausted, "they'll be even happier out there. Please don't ask me about removing claws. I certainly would not do it, as it leaves them almost defenceless. Get a pen built, and let me know how they are getting on in two weeks time!"

` After what I thought was good advice, I escaped to the car, unsure just how much Julie would do to rectify the situation. Arriving back at the surgery I scribbled in a revisit to check up on progress in ten days time when I would be on holiday. I felt that it was only right that Brian, as the senior member, should see Julie and give her the benefit of his vast experience. He might be safe if he could only be a bit brusque and leave his pheromones at home. I did feel some what guilty as I suspected that the privilege would fall to Mary.

The surgery had been fairly busy when Brian popped his head around the door, "Come on in for a cup of tea before you go home, Ned. I have a proposition for you!"

With that brief comment he left my curiosity hanging up in the air with my brain quietly muttering, what? when and why? Surely not another lady friend after his recent escape!"

I ushered in the next client who strutted in, exuding self confidence. A large brindle greyhound with a wide leather collar with brass studs around his neck, walked quietly at his side as if indifferent to his master's posing. He probably realised that he was needed as a status symbol to support his master's ego.

"Good evening," I said, "And what's your problem?"

In a broad Scots accent he replied, "I wannae have my running dawg vaccinated, in case she picks up this hard pad disease!"

I looked up from my desk where I had been writing and summed up the client. He was a small, dark man in his early thirties, sharp-featured, with black hair sleeked back with Brycreem in a fashion that I always associated with croupiers in casinos. He wore a red check shirt with open neck and rolled up sleeves which showed an almost simian expanse of thick black hair covering his arms and chest.

I hesitated for a moment as I tried to translate the accent. Playing for time I said, "Right, let's have a look at him. Has he been vaccinated before?"

"He's no had any jabs." came the terse reply as if challenging further comment.

The dog stood very quietly as I examined him and injected him with the vaccine. I started to fill out his vaccination certificate and casually asked details of his age and address. "What's your name?" I said, scratching the dog's head.

"Och. I'm Jimmie McLoughlin."

"Oh no! Sorry! but I was talking to the dog"

"Och, ye'd never know how to spell it!" Said Jimmie, quietly gloating over the ignorance of the Sassenach. "We call him Srianach."

"Oh!" I replied, "that's very logical as Srianach means 'the brindle one! Where did you pick up that name?"

Deflated, Jimmie's jaw dropped open in amazement and he momentarily forgot to keep posing particularly as this was the only Gaelic word that he knew. "Er, I got it from my granny, in Glasgow"

"Good for her," I said, smugly. "Tell her that you've met someone else, who has the Gaelic! I've not seen you before", I continued as I took down his details. "Are you working over here for the season?" I had learned, from experience, to be a bit careful about giving credit to non-residents, who might leave overnight.

"Aye, I'm a chef in the Sefton Hotel and I'm living with my sister Jeannie Quirk in Albany Street. Otherwise I wouldn't be able to keep my running dog."

I knew Jeannie fairly well as an attractive and voluptuous lass who helped out behind the bar in The Jolly Farmer. I had a bit of trouble tying in her happy character with this cocky wee man.

He left the room a much more subdued young man and, when he came in several times after that episode, Srianach was always introduced as granny's dawg!

Dave Quilleash farmed out at Ballelby, near Niarbyl. This area in the wild west always intrigued me as it was not far away from Doarlish Cashen, which was reputed to be haunted by Gef, a talking mongoose. It was reputed to speak several languages and repeat nursery rhymes. Voirrey, the daughter of the house, who was Dave's maternal aunt, claimed to have spoken to Gef the mongoose. There the trail ran cold.

I had always intended to visit Doarlish Cashen in the hope that I would find some evidence of this mythical beast as we didn't often meet a mongoose in the Island. However, tramping up amongst the ruins on a mizzly day with thick shrouds of mist swirling in across the moors was not my idea of a jolly day out.

Dave was a tall thin man, pale and stooped, who gave the impression that he would hardly survive a week against the raging storms which could batter this coast during the winter. Despite this, he would be out lamping for rabbits at night and checking his snares. He was very involved with nature and in his quiet manner would delight me with tales of all the bird life along the cliffs. He developed a faraway look as he described the choughs which frequented the cliffs and would drag me to the cliff edge to watch the antics of the clowns of the sky and listen to their soft 'chirr-chirr'.

He called to ask if I would look at a litter of piglets for him, "Same as last time", he said. "A bit lame" which suggested 'Glasser's Disease. This condition is caused by a bacteria present on many farms and causes stiffness and respiratory problems, but it is made worse by stressful conditions.

I called in at Ballellby fairly early, on my journey down towards Port St Mary. As I drew up in the yard there was no sign of anyone about so I walked around the pigs' house where I could see him bent over beside the sheep pens.

At the sound of my footsteps he half turned around-"Thank goodness you're here Ned. I've made an awful mess here!" His voice was almost breaking with emotion. "I found this old broken-mouth ewe with a broken leg about an hour ago and brought her home. She is worth nothin' so I decided to put her down painlessly with my .22

rifle. I shot her in the front of the skull twice and all she did was cry out and start bleeding. What's wrong. Is it the bullets is dud?"

I could see he was upset - almost in tears as every animal counted to this gentle man. "Sit down and I shall do it for you". I said firmly. Raising the rifle I placed the end of the barrel low behind the head and squeezed the trigger. The ewe dropped where she stood. Farmers have to deal with life and death as part of their occupation but become very concerned about the welfare of those animals in their care!

"It's like this Dave. If you try to shoot between the eyes, the bullet is liable to hit and ricochet off a thick pad of bone lying in front of the brain. An inch and a half higher and she would have died instantly. I was not taking chances with so much blood around, so shot her through the base of the skull. You weren't to know of the problem unless you were a slaughterman or a vet and you tried to do what was right. Now let's cast an eye on these piglets!"

As we entered the piggery there was a scuttling and grunting as the piglets rushed into the corner of the pens. Four pens held piglets of varying ages but it wasn't hard to see the affected animals by themselves. They were listless and walked around stiffly like toy soldiers. "It looks like Glassers disease alright. You've had several litters before, if I recall correctly."

"Yes!" responded Dave. "I had a batch of weaners earlier in the year. Why am I getting this suddenly?"

"Look at this one!" I added. "He's warm with a temperature, and his joints are swollen and painful. It's an infection they pick up if they're under stress. Often it occurs with the stress of weaning, but in your case I feel that there are other factors. I was noticing as I came in that the piggery is the least up-to-date part of your farm.

"If you can stand back and look at it as an outsider you will see that there are slates missing in the roof, gutters are broken and leaking down the walls-letting damp soak through. The doors and windows could benefit from a bit of loving care as the wind whistles inside. Just watch and I'll set a light to a wisp of straw."

Gathering some straw I lit a match and crouched down to floor level in the pen with the straw burning. "See-the smoke rises to the edge of the pen and is then blown away. Put yourself in the piglets' situation. You are lying on a damp bed with a cold draught blowing through the pen. Would you like to sleep in damp sheets? All this adds up to stress which allows the germs causing Glasser's disease to flourish in the piglets and stunt their growth or kill them. If you get to work and sort out draughts and damp, the little ones will be able to snuggle up together in a warm bed of straw. Don't forget to concrete in the holes in the floor so that urine can't collect in them and smell the place out as well as being a source of infection. There's a hole in that corner you could almost lose a whole litter in! Then you'll find that the troubles should cease. In the meantime, I shall inject them and hope for a rapid cure."

It had rained fairly steadily all day and the roads were awash in several places as I drove across the Island. On entering the surgery I was met at the door by Ruth. Pushing a couple of bottles of calcium into my hand she brusquely gave me my marching orders. "Can you go straight to see Jim Kennaugh at Grenaby. He's found a cow flat out with milk fever, could have been like it all night! I told him to sit her up and put bales behind her. He said that it would be mighty difficult as she's lying in the river!"

As I turned in my tracks and headed back for the car my mind was in a whirl. How on earth do I cope with a milk fever case in the water. All sorts of possible problems flashed through my mind.

At that moment I met Brian, who was returning from an early morning call. His cough had disappeared and he had a spring in his step once more. Almost reminiscent of another woman in his life!

I was not relishing the thought of standing out in the pouring rain, in a river and feeling damp for the rest of my morning calls. By the time that I reached Ballasalla, the weather gods had relented, the sun had appeared to banish the rain and left the whole air sparkling and vibrant for twenty minutes until the next black cloud.

Jim Kennaugh's smallholding consisted of a few grey stone buildings backing onto the road with a gate opening into the farmyard, flanked by a concrete stand for his milk churns. As I stepped out of the car, Juan, Jim's son, appeared out of the turnip house. "Good morning Mr Carson. Dad told me to keep an eye open for you. I'll take you down the field to the cow. We didn't expect old Bess to calve down last night, she wasn't made up at all."

Clad in our water-proofs, we collected our gear and hurried down the paddock, heads bent into the wind and driving rain, which had returned with a vengeance. The land sloped downwards towards the line of sycamores and thorn trees bordering the stream. As we hurried down towards the bottom corner of the field, I could see an old grey Ferguson tractor and three figures huddled under the trees for shelter.

I couldn't see Bess until I was within ten yards. Only her head was visible above the swirling waters, supported by a halter tied to the nearest tree.

My heart sank. I couldn't recall the textbooks describing this situation and certainly our extramural studies in Crowe's bar never produced a similar situation. How on earth do you inject into the jugular vein when the cow is largely under water? A quick plea to my maker for first aid! For sure, to drag Bess out of the river using tractor and manpower would kill the old girl, as she looked pretty far gone already.

Hastily, I handed Juan the open calcium bottle whilst I attached the rubber cap of the flutter valve tubing.

I stepped into the flooded stream, hypodermic needle in hand, only to end up crutch high in the cold muddy water.

Urgency ruled. "Juan, come and stand beside me and turn the bottle upside down when I ask. Jim, when I say so, can the three of you raise Bess's head out of the water so that I can get the needle into the vein. Don't let go, mind!"

As I stood poised, like a whale hunter waiting for the kill, they lifted her, exposing the neck and I harpooned the needle into the neck. Fortune favours the bold, bull's eye first time and blood jetted out of the needle. Attaching the rubber tubing connection, I held the needle in place just as the lifting gang tired and gently lowered her neck back into the muddy torrent.

"My God," exclaimed Jim. "That was a mighty good shot, yessir! You must've spent time practising at the dart board in the Jolly Farmer."

Feeling somewhat flattered I muttered, "It could be that Jim but think of all those years of training at college learning to throw the javelin! That's what you're paying for!"

Rather thrown by this remark, Jim stood watching as I observed the calcium level in the bottle slowly dropping. Each millilitre slowly increased Bess's chances of survival. After about ten minutes of slow administration we managed to sit Bess up in the stream, much to our relief. We stood back to consider our next move as the poor animal was suffering from hypothermia and would probably die of cold if she remained in the water. I realised just how cold I felt as I had been standing in the river up to my waist.

Bess solved part of our dilemma by attempting, vainly, to get onto her feet. Juan was sent off for a length of cart rope. Putting two men on each end, we passed it around her rump. Each time she struggled with her front legs, we pulled and gradually eased her onto the bank, where she sat, trembling and bewildered.

Jim and Juan went off to the yard and shortly afterwards returned with Mary, the Clydesdale mare, pulling the farm cart laden with hay bales and a couple of tarpaulins. We pulled Bess on to a tarpaulin and rubbed her down vigorously with a wad of hay to dry her off and then covered her in a bed of hay before adding another tarpaulin to keep in the warmth in the manner of a string vest.

"I'll give her another bottle of calcium Jim, if you can drench her every hour with a pint of strong coffee. I will also leave you some Nux Stimulant powders to drench her with three times a day. Don't leave them around, because they're poisonous to the dogs! As we are all pretty well drenched, I suggest that we go home and change into something dry. Mind you, the guy who draws the short straw must stay with her, as she could fall into the river again. I'll be back after lunch."

As we removed our waterproofs in the turnip shed, Jim's wife Anne, appeared with mugs of steaming hot tea. She took one look at me and said, "My dear Mr Carson, I shall fetch you a pair of Jim's trousers and a shirt to go home in, otherwise you'll end up with pneumonia." With that she disappeared and returned with some old clothes.

"Now, put those on you for the journey home or your wife will be very cross."

Feeling cold and miserable, I drove home wondering where the glamour of veterinary practice had gone. Moira was shopping in Douglas so I rushed straight upstairs and into a hot bath and lay back to warm up, as I munched a couple of jam sandwiches. I felt much more human after a change of clothes and a mug of tea, and headed down south once more to Grenaby.

Thankfully, the weather had started to improve. The grey skies were being rolled back by puffy white cumulus interspersed with patches brilliant blue sky. After the rain, the air was fresh and vibrant. As I headed down the field the sunlight glittered, like so many cats eyes, in the rain sodden sward.

The Kennaugh family were gathered around the recumbent Bess. She was looking much more alert, her ears pricked, and as I slid my hand under the tarpaulin she felt warm and dry.

"She's struggled a bit," said Jim, "but is still unable to stand. If we leave her here tonight, she could well end up in the river again."

"If you have a partly empty Dutch barn," I interjected, "we could put her in there and give her some shelter. She's not in an easy spot here, but how do we get her up there?"

"There is an old barn door in the yard that we were going to use as firewood," said Juan. "If we put the cart rope through the air vents at the top and tie it to the back of the tractor we could pull her up on it!"

"Good idea!" I replied. "Get some of the neighbours in to help, tie her feet together and roll her onto the door. Put a halter on her and have one man holding her head down. If the head can't move she should lie quiet. Take her slowly up the hill; and bed her down well in the shed. I shall drop in tomorrow."

"Goodbye and thanks Ned," said Jim looking much happier. "She means a lot to us as a cow and a source of income. She is nearly twenty per cent of our herd!"

The Kennaugh family were always so welcoming when I called in, that I would often squeeze their call into my round. They taught me so much about basic stockmanship and the TLC factor. It is folks like this that make large animal practice so enjoyable. Each cow was a member of the family with their own name, and each received more care and attention when they were off colour than many people I knew.

It was a strict routine that one of the men would stay out in the loosebox to look after the ailing animal, keep a rug on her for warmth with an ample supply of water and feed such as cabbage or turnips with a bit of ivy as an appetizer. If the animal was recumbent, she had to be rolled from side to side every two hours in order to avoid pneumonia.

If there was a suggestion of pneumonia before the advent of antibiotics I would ask for a pot of mustard and some brown paper. The mustard was spread over the brown paper and this was laid over the chest wall and then the animal was wrapped in a rug. The object of this 'rubifacient' was to mildly inflame the skin over the ribs, increasing the blood flow and removing infection as well as keeping the patient warm. This was repeated daily.

With all this attention in the loosebox the farmer also needed sustenance with a flask of tea and sandwiches.

I can recall having a mustard plaster to my own chest when I nearly died from pneumonia! It is all quite vague as I lost six weeks of my life during my illness as I regularly lapsed from consciouness back into a dreamy detached state.

People and their interactions with animals never fail to fascinate me, and watching the results of these encounters has always been a source of great pleasure. One of the greatest challenges in veterinary practice is the subtle relationship between children and animals. Both can be delightful, horrid and noisy but always capable of cutting you down to size. If a child has been brought up to respect animals a mutual trust can arise.

It was my surgery duty and the waiting room was crowded with the sick lame and lazy. I had spent the day on the farms in the pouring rain and had looked forward to this session in the warmth.

The first client to arrive was Milo Cusick and his mother, recently arrived from Ireland. One look at this young sixteen-year old set alarm bells ringing. Dressed in a tattered old suit, which must have been someone else's cast-offs, he looked extremely scruffy. The manner in which he was constantly drawing his sleeve across his snotty nose, with his spiky black hair, pointing every which way as if he had used a garden rake to groom himself didn't improve his appearance. He dragged a hessian sack behind him that seemed to progress in a series of leaps.

His mother, a tiny wee woman, well wrapped up in a worn black coat, trotted along at his side looking down at the ground, face half hidden, as if she were in purdah.

"Good evening!" I greeted him brightly, to cover up my surprise. "What have you got in the bag for me today?"

"It's moi cat, mister," uttered Milo in his broad Dublin accent, "He needs to be dressed." He looked down at the sack that was rolling across the floor, as if his cat normally behaved in such a fashion.

"Er, dressing is it," I mumbled to hide my confusion. "Has he cut his leg then? When did it happen?"

Milo's mum turned her head towards me so that I could just see a pair of glittering eyes from the depths of the coat and a sharp nasal whine, like a catarrhal banshee shot out "Do yer not know? You've got our Milo wrong, mister. The stinkin' little heller needs his knackers cut off!"

Taken aback by the explicit detail I hesitated, and then remembered the expression from my college days, but was left wondering whether "little heller" referred to Milo or the cat!

"Jasus, Mister! I remember you," interrupted Milo. "You treated Poncho, that old flea bag of a pony belonging to me Da! It was about this time two years ago that we brought him up ter the vitinry college in Ballsbridge. My father said that the craitur would never get better because you spoke posh like the bloody Black an' Tans, and wouldn't know what you were doin'! And him fightin' for freedom during the troubles"

Then it dawned on me. Father and son had arrived at a clinic in the college with their pony and cart, which they used in the rag and bone trade. A good thing that Poncho hadn't worn clothes or he would have been as scruffy as his owners. They were hard times in Dublin when many people existed well below the poverty line. This was evident by the condition of the pony, which was completely emaciated and sunken-eyed with pus streaming from his nose. His sides were heaving from the exertion of being driven up the road. Even the pieces of leatherwork on his harness were held together with pieces of string.

"Yes, I replied. I remember. Your father was not very pleased to meet what he thought was an Englishman and gave me the full story about the Easter rising. It was only when I told him that most of the V.C.'s in the war were won by Irishmen that he quietened down. Your pony had strangles and pneumonia, if I remember correctly. How did he go on?"

"Oh sir. It was a different story when he recovered almost overnight. He only needed one more treatment. Every night father would stagger home from Mooney's bar singing 'The Risin' of the Moon' or some such republican song, and him after telling all his drinking pals about the wonderful English professor who looked after Poncho, and the amazing way in which he injected a great syringeful of stuff into her jugular vein. And her standing as quiet and calm as a lady in spite of being on the verge of dyin'. My God. I tink that he has got your name down for a sainthood!"

"Where is your father now, Milo?"

"Oh he's back in Dublin still. We ran away from home. Me, mother and little Diarmuid. He just couldn't keep away from the drink. Any money he earned was spent in the pub and then he would reel in drunk, pukin' all over the place, and if mother complained he beat her almost insensible. The very next day he would be at confession asking for forgiveness. God might well smile upon him, but we couldn't live under those conditions, so I saved up the fare and brought the family over here to escape. I hope to God he never finds us."

Rather upset by their story I changed the subject.

"Let me have a look at him Milo," I continued, "We shall probably need to keep him in overnight."

Milo heaved the sack unceremoniously onto the table, untied the cord, and plunged his arm inside. Like a conjurer with a white rabbit, he lifted out an enormous ginger tom cat.

"Der you are vitinry. Dat's Feeney, who is gettin' a bit out of hand and needs dressin'!"

Not only was Feeney large but he had eyes like a couple of green saucers constantly watching me from a turnip size head. To add to his charms he had ears sliced into sections by attacking claws and a number of wounds on his face made him appear rather moth eaten. Sure enough he had an odour that only a lovelorn pussy cat could appreciate.

"Now that is some cat Milo. He must be three or four years old. Why did you call him Feeney?"

"Yis mister. He's all of tree years and a lovely animal all right, but he does keep killing the neighbours' cats. We called him after Dan Joe Feeney who came courtin' my sister, Siobhan, in Dublin. He had red hair, green eyes and a great appetite for the wimmen. Mind you, I thought he smelled a bit worse than the cat."

"You must excuse me mam being all wrapped up like, but he pee'd on the floor and as she grabbed him to put him in the sack he took a hold of her face with his claws, and she bled somethin' terrible."

Feeling very guilty I took Feeney in for his operation, realising that this would be the end of an illustrious career.

22

One of Mary's most redeeming features was her self confidence and ability to remain cool under pressure. This was evident when we sent her off to carry out her first TB test at Peter Quirk's farm where I had started the previous year. Of course the weather had been so terrible that a repeat of last year was very unlikely!

It had rained for twenty-four hours previously. We had taken the precaution of enrolling the assistance of Roy and Val Callin in the hope of organising the operation, as they too had fought hard to build up their farm when they started. The other asset was that the test would be supervised by no less than Duggie Kerruish, the Chief Veterinary Officer. Despite all the precautions their plans were doomed to go awry.

Mary arrived promptly at 9a.m. with Duggie Kerruish as her supervisor. The leaden sky was filled with foreboding and plummeting rain streamed across the yard in torrents.

The usual chaos ensued. Cattle, being driven in from the hill with their calves, scattered across the fields and found escape holes through the hedges, leaving the soaked drovers floundering up to their knees in mud.

We had planned and talked a lot during the year, and in the yard Peter had constructed a holding pen from which he could drive six animals at a time into a chute ending in a crush, with a yoke to hold the animal still for ear tattooing and testing. In theory this was the ultimate system and should work perfectly!

For Peter this was a labour of love as he had become engaged to Mavis Quirk, a distant relative from Raby farm. She had challenged him to make the farm work before they got married. They had worked hard all summer erecting new field gates, cleaning out cowsheds, and boarding across windows, which might provide bolt holes. There was also the problem of building a milking parlour, concreting out the yard, and renovating buildings to make them fit for livestock.

The test was a big improvement on the previous year, if the weather factor was excluded. Mary carried out the test most efficiently despite her sou'wester and oilskins. Unfortunately, inky fingers and driving rain successfully smeared all the recorded entries. Duggie Kerruish assisted admirably, but as the morning progressed he was heard to comment several times, "I don't think that Josie Corkish will like this very much!"

By lunchtime it was all over, the sky had dried up and sunbeams tentatively shone through the grey sky, with the promise of a nice evening.

Mavis and Peter, sighing with relief, produced flasks of hot tea and scones for the cold and hungry workers. Whilst they sat on hay bales congratulating themselves on the improved facilities Peter recounted the saga of Uncle Ebenezer for Mary's benefit. She almost believed that Ebenezer had been pushed into the flooded river and drowned by the little people, whilst Roy kept nodding and saying that his uncle knew Ebenezer well! Val turned to Mary, laughingly, and said, "My dear Mary. Don't you believe all their tales. Neither Roy nor Peter know what the truth is! Anythin' for a good story if you can practice keepin' a straight face!"

When she arrived back in the evening, Brian smiled with satisfaction "Mary! Get yourself ready for the government rottweiler, when she tells you off after receiving your test report. Still, we have three days to get you into training. Sure enough, within twenty four hours of the test reports being sent in, the peace of the morning was shattered by the shrill ringing of the 'phone.

Mary, chuckling, took the call whilst we all watched in anticipation. "Good morning, Mrs Corkish! I'm Mary Sutherland. I believe that you wish to speak to me."

Josie's staccato response crackled on the line. "Yes, Miss Sutherland. I most certainly do. I have been examining your test reports from Quirk, 'The Lhergy', and they leave a lot to be desired. The forms are untidy, smudged with ink and speckled with cow dung. This really will not do, and you must improve your standards, as I shall have to mention this to Mr Kerruish."

By this time Mary was beside herself with a mixture of irritation and joy. Indeed, she had to sit down at the table to collect herself ready for her reply. I had never seen her mood change so rapidly.

"Mrs Corkish! she commenced in a frigid tone. "I have been TB testing in Yorkshire for three years without complaint. My test at Quirk 'The Lhergy' was carried out in extreme conditions, under the supervision of Mr Duggie Kerruish. Indeed, you will find that some of the recording is in his handwriting. Do mention it to Mr Kerruish and he can share his experience with you. As it appears that you have no practical experience of testing, may I suggest that you join me next week and carry out the recording duties, at which you will probably be highly proficient! It may assist your appreciation of on farm problems. I shall be talking to Mr Kerruish later in the day. Good day Mrs Corkish and thank you for calling!

After replacing the receiver she collapsed into a chair and asked for a cup of tea with two lumps of sugar, whilst we burst into applause and laughter.

Brian's face was a wondrous sight. He was red faced and spluttering with mirth. "Good for you Mary. I felt quite sorry for Josie. You are hereby appointed as the practice dragon slayer. Oh! To be a fly on the wall in the office at the moment!"

At lunchtime, Duggie called in on his way home to hear our side of the story. Apparently he had arrived in the office to find Josie incandescent with rage, and the junior clerks, heads down riveted to their work. She was holding a broken telephone handset. "Mr Kerruish!" she raged. "never have I been spoken to in such a manner. That awful Miss Sutherland almost laughed at my attempt to correct her sloppy presentation. I have a good mind to resign from this office and change to another government department!"

"Oh!" responded Duggie , "I know that the problem was unavoidable and I was supervising Miss Sutherland's testing. Despite everything we finished early. Perhaps you would like to spend a day with one of the vets to see their problems first hand. Mind you if you are intent on changing departments, I shall recommend you highly!"

At this stage, almost screaming with fury, Josie swept out of the office, slamming the door behind her, and leaving her juniors in a fit of the giggles.

"Well!" continued Duggie chuckling quietly "It looks as if I shall have to promote one of the juniors to fill Josie's shoes. Shall we drink to it! I don't think you are that frightening Mary are you?"

The next day a curt note arrived at the Board of Agriculture office explaining to Duggie that Josie was taking a week off to consider her position, as it appeared that the administration in the Animal Health office was falling to pieces and in addition her efforts were not fully appreciated!

It was indeed a solemn moment as the clerical staff were overjoyed and Voirrey Joughin, the senior clerk was asked to fill Josie's position until her return.

The good news was not long in arriving as after a few days, Josie informed Duggie that she was transferring to the Social Services department, where the opportunities for promotion were unlimited for an experienced person.

Duggie's other claim to fame was his abiding interest in Manx cats and the reason for them being tailess. Many variations occur. There are 'rumpies',the true Manxie, which has no residue of a tail and 'stumpies' whose tail can range from one inch to a definite external tail'

At this time there was interest from the University of Newcastle who were trying to correlate 'Manxness' with spinabifida in humans. This all came to nought in the end. There is no such thing as a pedigree Manx cat as the gene mutation for Manxness is a lethal factor. Inbreeding Manx cats can result in progressively less vertebrae until there are no vertebrae in the pelvis and the animal becomes paralysed. I had proof of this with my own little cat 'Manninagh Beg' who produced a litter of kittens. After a couple of days we were constantly finding one kitten deposited in the litter tray. I watched her repeatedly carrying the youngster to the tray and dumping her there. It was only on examination that I discovered that the kitten had no vertebrae in the pelvis and would not be able to walk. 'Manninagh' in her wisdom realised that the kitten did not behave correctly and disposed of her as a reject!

One of the endearing features of Manx cats is their good nature. Many of them possess a double coat like a rabbit, and they do not have the ability to kill birds as easily as their normal cousins. This is probably as a result of their long back legs, which makes it more awkward to stalk or run on level ground. Their preferred means of attack, often, is to leap in the air and drop onto their prey. They are, however, very good mousers and bring home many young rabbits.

Shortly after this episode we moved into Douglas once more, to stay with mum and dad, as time grew short and the baby was due. Better than if we lived at home, lest I was not available when this much awaited addition arrived. My great ambition was to be there at the birth for our second child but nature intervened as I developed a nasty skin infection as well as contracting brucellosis. As a result I could not even cuddle my daughter Alison until I was completely cured.

The brucellosis (Contagious Abortion in cattle or Undulant Fever in humans) was not as simple to cure, and remained with me causing several years of depression before the symptoms settled down. The human form results in fluctuating fever, muscle and joint pains, as well as depression. I was fortunate that it was diagnosed and treated early with specific antibiotics, which allayed most of the symptoms but I had eight years of depression ahead of me. The disease is picked up by contact with discharges, after an infected cow calves or drinking unpasteurised milk.

March had been a mild month and the work was quiet. The baby's arrival was imminent and everything was becoming an effort for Moira so my assistance was always welcome and I tried to be at home as much as possible to care for our son, Donal, who was now two years old.

At the end of the month our dream was fulfilled. Alison arrived to make up the pigeon pair. She was a delight to behold, blue eyed and fair skinned like her mother. Her big brother was entranced by her, and for the first year he kept her supplied with toys. Her wish was his command to such an extent that she felt it unnecessary to stand or walk whilst she had waiter service, and consequently was very late in walking. Little did we realise that this placid child would end up as a globe trotter!

As Mary settled in to the practice she started to organise her own work and developed her own following of clients. One particular character, Ernie Quilliam, kept a few cattle and sheep on a small holding above Laxey. He took a shine to her and on the pretext that she had small hands suited to delivering lambs easily, and demanded her services regularly. The farm was quite a ramshackle affair, with a cobbled cow house where he hand milked half-a-dozen cows, which by the standards of the time was above subsistence level. He and his son George also had about 50 ewes grazing the hill pastures below Windy Corner, overlooked by the Snaefell Railway.

It was on these wild hills dotted with bracken and wild daffodils that Dad and I spent many hours hunting for rabbits to feed the dogs which also had the added bonus of controlling myxomatosis.

Whenever Mary was called in to a lambing or calving Ernie would send his mousy little wife, Mildred, indoors to make some tea and scones for the vetinary. "It's not right for wimmen to be seein' such things." he would mutter. Quite where that put Mary we never worked out.

When she called at the farm one day Ernie stared at her and said, "You work too hard, Miss Sutherland! All work and no play is no good. I'll tell 'ee what! I'll take you out for a drink one evening and we can have some fun."

Mary, looking delighted, said. "What a good idea Mr Quilliam. There's only one small problem as I only drink double scotch but after a few of those I could enjoy my evening! I shall look forward to that!"

Ernie took a deep breathe, as he had only visualised buying half a pint and rapidly changed the subject. The story did cause us a lot of mirth when we met later.

This was not to be Mary's last challenge at the Quilliam household. One lovely summer evening as the sun was slanting down across the western hills she was called out to visit a calf with respiratory problems. As the car drew into the yard she tooted the horn to announce her presence in case the menfolk were working in the fields. After a couple of minutes the large shambling figure of George appeared. "G'd evening George! What a lovely day it's been! Springtime makes the birds and bees feel good!" was her greeting. "Where's this poorly calf?"

"Look in here Miss!" replied George. "Sorry it's a bit low. It's only an old converted piggery."

As Mary entered she gasped, in the darkness, as the acrid urine, filled air struck her eyes. "Can't you get a bit of air flow through here. The ventilation pipes are all blocked up with straw, No wonder the calf has problems. They are all of your own making. Take out all this straw, get some air flow and light so that the calf can live comfortably."

George fumbled and pulled out the straw filling. At once light and fresh air flowed into the shed.

Mary put her hand on the calf's back which was dripping with moisture. "No wonder the poor creature's in trouble. All this saturated air lies on the galvanised roof and when the cool night air hits it, condensation drops on the calf's back and look," she continued, "this bedding is sodden. Would you like to lie in bed, if you had peed in it? That's the cause of his pneumonia!"

George, taken aback by too much information could only `stand back and think. "Ah Miss! Father said to block up the holes to keep the calves warm. I see now, it's the 'compensation' that makes them sick. I shall change the bedding tonight."

"I'll just inject the calf and see him again tomorrow, in the hope that the air will be much fresher." At this point Mary went out to the car and returned with a syringe loaded with antibiotic.

Whether it was her mastery of the situation or the talk of the birds and bees in the springtime we shall never know, but as she bent towards the calf Mary felt a large hairy arm slip around her waist. Momentarily, she hesitated, and her elbow jerked hard backwards, accompanied by a gasp of pain and intake of air from George. Calmly she turned around and said. "George, if you try that once more this needle goes straight up your arse!"

George turned as white as a sheet, and sat on the wall outside sadly contemplating the unfairness of life as Mary concluded brusquely "I'll see you in the morning!"

The last client in the waiting room was Mary Cowley whose spaniel, Jane, had been so ill with distemper last year. They came in casually to report progress. Jane had recovered almost completely but had been left with chorea, or St. Vitus Dance, which can appear in many forms. Jane's affliction was a constant frown and movement of her ears of which she was unaware. It was quite comical to see Jane being affectionate whilst her ears were continually jumping up and down.

An emergency had just arrived from the Trafalgar boarding house on the promenade. Many of these houses had large kitchens to feed their hungry guests. Mrs Quayle, the owner was sobbing on the phone. "Oh! Mr Carson, can you come quickly please? Our old Persian cat 'Molly' has disappeared and we are afraid that, as she loves her comfort, she may have crept into the oven in the range seeking warmth."

"Certainly Mrs Quayle I shall come at once and see what I can do. Give me five minutes!"

'The Trafalgar' was one of the large double fronted buildings facing Douglas Bay so I rang the front doorbell as I entered, realising that everyone would be fairly busy. There was a bark and scrabbling of feet in the corridor, and hurtling towards me appeared a Pembroke corgi. Without further ado, he launched into space and bit me on the navel as a welcome greeting. I went downstairs to the kitchen and found one of the staff, a young lady in her teens. "Hello! I've come to help to trace Molly. Have you found her yet?"

"No," came the choked response,"but we think that she is in here!" pointing to one of the lower ovens. I knelt down and reached into the open door and sure enough I could feel the body of a cat at the back. Unfortunately, Molly had sauntered into the lukewarm oven the previous evening and somebody had closed the door as part of the routine. I called for a cardboard box and gently curled up the body inside for the journey back to the surgery.

I had never handled mink. They had not been mentioned in our college curriculum and my student amours were not in the financial bracket to have rubbed shoulders with mink stoles!

Charles Romilly, recently demobbed from the RAF and living in Ballasalla, decided that mink farming was the new, profitable occupation and that if he could breed and sell mink to supply the fur farmers he could make lots of money without the messy problem of slaughtering them for their pelts.

There was very little knowledge available about the diseases of mink although it was just emerging that they could die with canine distemper. Brian decided, in his wisdom, that as I was a recent graduate that I should look into the matter whilst Mary pleaded an allergy to the species. I might even become an authority in mink medicine?

Mink are members of the Mustelid family, which classifies them with stoats, ferrets, weasels, otters, and even badgers. This means that they are strong, agile carnivores with very sharp teeth!

We had to develop handling techniques before the advent of crush cages by the use of heavy leather gloves. We treated various problems such as bites, abscesses and canine distemper. One female called Mata Hari was always in trouble. Instead of fighting with tooth and claw she always obliged by fainting, just long enough to enable us to carry out treatment before she recovered. My only other contact with the family was going out rabbiting with ferrets who always came across as friendly and placid.

Tragedies occur in veterinary practice despite all the loving care bestowed upon our charges. There are always reports of cattle and sheep falling over cliffs but fortunately these are few and far between. We had not reached the 'animal rights' era when mindless people felt that it was clever and compassionate to release potentially dangerous carnivores.

In mink farming, despite their ultimate fate, the animals were fed well and euthanased humanely. When a farm was raided and all the mink released there was a concerted effort by farmers, wildfowlers and government to eliminate them, as they had difficulty surviving in the wild. What did suffer from the mink were, cats, ducks, poultry, water voles and our native wildlife. So much for free expression! How fortunate that they did not find their way into a new-born baby's pram!

Variations from routine help to make practice life extremely interesting. We had to treat wallabies and storks on several occasions. We were working in the dark as the owners didn't know how to restrain them and the dosage of drugs was very much guesswork. Little did I realise at the time just how pet interests would change, and me with them.

Pat and Michael Robson were both the only children of comfortable middle class families and, as such, had been cushioned through boarding school neither the guidance nor pressure to achieve in business or academically. Apart from each other, their common interest was in horses and the open air. She was very competent in the show-jumping ring whilst he acted as her groom. The logical future was to buy land for the horses and, as he had spent many happy times working on his uncle's dairy farm at Ballamaddrell, they persuaded the family to invest in a farm near Garwick. They bought a unit of nearly a hundred acres from Tommy Kewin, a distant cousin of Michael's father, who wanted to spend his retirement quietly in Laxey. It was good pasture backing up towards the hills with quite ramshackle buildings which had been neglected as Tommy had given up cattle in preference to sheep as anno domini caught up on him.

Pat and Mike set to with great enthusiasm repairing gates and fences. In a moment of midsummer madness, they bought twenty in-calf Ayrshire heifers and thirty Dorset Horn sheep, which meant that they had to have their dairy constructed before the heifers calved down.

The old buildings were a major repair project as they required new doors and windows and concreted floors. They attacked the project with great energy. Pat was the planner and builder's labourer whilst Michael did the heavy carrying and digging. They opted for a line-abreast parlour so that the cows would come in batches of six and milk was carried away by pipeline into the dairy to ease the labour of carrying churns back and forth. This was all very modern and the family helped them out financially.

Despite a winter of variable weather, they managed to finish the dairy setup and cattle collecting yard with a few months to spare, before the first cows calved. They got down to the lambing and finished off with a good yield from their first lamb crop. Pat had tiny hands, which helped with delivering the lambs.

With all this industry, Pat suddenly realised that she had a bump of her own. It must have been the all the hormones being produced that put her in the mood. However, she didn't let this interfere with her pleasure on the farm. Once the lambing had finished she was helping Michael with the calvings.

The confinement for Pat was very straight-forward and with only a short delay they were both milking again. The baby's pram had a special space in the dairy so that she could supervise milking and the child.

On a warm spring evening the phone rang and Pat's voice, sounding quite serious said, "Ned! I'm glad it's you. We need some help with a calving heifer. There doesn't appear to be any passage for the calf to come through! Her waters have broken but she isn't really straining as much as she should. Can you come out to see her please? We shall have a pail of warm water, soap and a towel ready for you!"

"I'll be out as soon as I can! Can you get a neighbour in to help in case we might need some muscle, I don't want you overexerting yourself in your present state." It was always a delight to deal with such a straightforward and efficient lady.

I arrived about half an hour later. Michael had driven her into a loosebox with Tom Gearing, his neighbour, and tied her up ready for inspection. She looked almost normal, with a periodic effort at forcing. As I slipped my hand inside the vagina, I knew at once what the problem was. The vaginal wall was twisted round in an anticlockwise direction, restricting the aperture inside.

"Michael, somehow she has developed a twist or torsion of the vagina, and of course, rather like twisting the neck of a paper bag, the entrance has been narrowed right down and has prevented the calf entering the pelvis. We have two options. If I can reach the feet we may be able to rotate the womb back to normal, or we may have to roll her over on the ground, which is the hard way."

Inserting my arm further into the vagina I could just feel the tips of the calf's toes but not enough to grasp them firmly. "Now I would like Tom and yourself to stand on opposite sides of her belly. Tom on the left gets both his fists and pushes upwards and across and you on the right alternately push downwards and across. In this way you get a gentle rocking and twisting motion on the uterus, and I shall have my hand inside and try to twist the neck of the cervix. If you can get a rhythmical movement we may succeed."

The men set to and there was no immediate response but slowly the aperture into the uterus opened. This was most exciting to me, and I was able to grasp both feet and fetlocks. "Take a rest now! I can see you're both grunting a little. My next move, as I can hold the feet, is to twist the fetlocks at right angle and use them as a lever to help to turn the calf. Right let's go again."

As we renewed our efforts the calf started to rotate and I was able to pull its feet into the pelvis. "All hands on deck. I'll put a calving rope on each foot, and if you could gently lean back and assist her as she strains, we should winkle this youngster out easily."

In no time a pretty little heifer calf was lying in the straw. I poked a piece of straw gently into her nostril to make her snort and bring up any mucus from her nostrils.

"Thanks!" commented Michael. "Our births have been problem free so far and it's always nice to know you're at hand even though you do cost money."

"We'll have another problem fairly soon. A year ago I bought a skittish young colt, Beau Geste, and haven't had time to break him in. He lets me put a halter on, because it means feed time but we've not got any further yet. He can use his feet when he feels inclined, so I don't want Pat going near him at the moment."

"He's going to need castrating fairly soon as he keeps falling in love with the neighbours mares, and regards a six-bar gate as a minor obstruction to courtship, so we might make a date fairly soon to have him deflowered!. It would do no harm to have some help as well. Don't bring Brian as Pat's in love with him! Better to have Mary before she gets gobbled up by a young farmer."

We eventually arranged a day about a week later, and I arrived with Mary to geld this rumbustious character. I had prayed for a sunny day and somehow my wishes were granted. Collecting all our gear in a wheel barrow, we walked down across the field with Michael to where a farm track ran between two fields, "We can halter him here" commented Michael. "There are hedges both sides of the lane to enclose him!"

He rattled the bucket with horse nuts and called out for Beau. A distant whinny and a thunder of hooves announced his arrival. He was a handsome bay with white socks, a broad blaze down his face, and a carefree look which indicated an independence of spirit. Already he was developing a deep neck to emphasise his masculinity. As he plunged his head into the bucket, Michael slipped a halter over his head with a length of lead rope attached to it.

"Hold on Michael" instructed Mary. "We shall try to get sidelines on him to cast him!" Michael was already having trouble restraining the restive colt and as soon as he saw the ropes, he backed away, reared, and struck out at Michael with his fore feet. Mary and I started to attach the sidelines as Beau' became increasingly restive, shifting from foot to foot. Michael hung on in an attempt to get some control, but Beau was having none of it. Again he pulled back, reared up, and went straight over backwards, dragging Michael after him. He hit the ground with a thud and then didn't stir!

As we rushed across, he took a breath and we could see that he was out for the count – absolutely pole-axed by a rock on which he hit his head as he fell. "Quickly get the side lines on him," I shouted and as Mary and Michael got to work I concentrated on the patient and found that he was breathing normally but unconscious. In no time, he was trussed up like a chicken, leaving Mary to watch the patient whilst Michael sat on his neck

I collected my instruments from the steriliser and disinfected the operative area. Incising the scrotum with the scalpel, I exposed both testicles and applied the emasculator to the testicular cord and blood vessels, which has the effect of crushing the tissue to prevent haemorrhage. I did take the extra precaution of putting a ligature on both sides above the emasculator as I didn't fancy coming back to treat Beau if there was any bleeding afterwards.

Standing back from the horse as we released the ropes Michael chuckled. "I have been dreading breaking him in, as he is such a handful, but as long as he has no permanent damage I can't think of a better time!" With that comment he rushed up to the stable and reappeared with girth saddle and bridle. Once he had the tack all on, we stood and watched as very slowly, a very confused horse sat up and wondered what had hit him. After ten minutes he stood up and let himself be led around by the reins and bridle. A further coaxing and talking by Michael, and we quietly helped him to mount and led Beau around in circles to get used to his new load. The result was most impressive and Michael called us two days later to let us know that he had quietly ridden Beau for a few minutes each day, and they were getting on very well.

I visited the farm fairly regularly once the heifers calved down and Pat who had produced a lovely flaxen haired daughter couldn't really give up her farm work and it was a regular sight to see the pram sitting outside the dairy whilst Pat was inside cleaning up the milking utensils or feeding the chickens.

The unexpected is always lurking around the corner in veterinary practice and is no respecter of class, rank or occasion. The summer had been very hot and sticky and the promenades were full of happy holiday makers soaking in the sun and splashing in the waters to cool off. The big band sound still echoed along Douglas promenade at nights.

Joe Loss filled the Villa Marina at night with the happy crowds swaying to the music and romancing beneath starlit skies. It always amazed me that such a sophisticated, smooth character should possess a red setter as a companion. Setters are a dream to work with as gundogs, but otherwise they can be dizzy redheads.

Ivy Benson and her all girl orchestra were very popular in the island, and she would appear in surgery regularly with her poodles for an 'M.O.T.' She had had to fight her way to the top in show business and I found her a delightfully direct lady.

Our other entertainment was Ronnie Aldrich and The Squadronaires who first met as a band in the RAF during the war and continued to entertain us at the Palace Ballroom, Douglas until the 1960s.

Brian went away on holiday in the early summer, and left Mary and me to hold the fort. During this time I was called on to examine a stork, which was being imported into the Curraghs Wildlife Park. I knew very little about stork health problems and but managed to impress the authorities that I had some expertise.

Shortly after this a circus arrived in Douglas much to the excitement of locals and holidaymakers. Performing lions were part of the act, so I managed to persuade Mary that I was allergic to circuses and she would have to carry out any necessary treatments. The morning arrived when a call came from the circus to attend some of the animals. Fortunately, I was away on an emergency and the privilege fell to Mary. I had just returned when she arrived back from her call.

"How did it go?" I inquired, trying to sound concerned.

"It wasn't too stressfull", came the response. "Of course I am fairly accomplished at coping with the exotic patients and all went very well. As you can see, I have no cuts or bruises." I immediately sensed that she was trying to score points, so I lost interest and changed the subject.

But she persisted, "You must surely want to know how I fared in the face of the circus animals"

"Alright, you win. Tell Dr Carson all about it!"

"It wasn't much really." she smiled slyly. "I was met by a most charming French gentleman, who thanked me so profusely for such rapid service, as he had visions of being unable to perform this evening!"

"Come on! I'm not interested in the trainer. How did you cope with the lions without being eaten?"

"To tell you the truth it was quite simple as I have this natural ability to sooth the savage beast!" At this point she could contain herself no longer, and started giggling. "The charming gentleman in question had a troupe of performing poodles and one of them had a cough. They all came bounding out and I said, these are not real French poodles!"

Not to be out done he said. 'Regardez mam'selle' Calling the poodles over he wagged his finger at them, said sharply 'Vous Asseyez vous!' and they all sat down. I think that he rather fancies me, as he gave me two tickets for the circus. I shall take Tom with me, as security"

The dog days of summer were upon us, when it is so hot that it is a pleasure to work indoors. And the farmers didn't call as they were all out working in the fields. Haymaking had been a bit hazardous as the rain kept interrupting the sun-drying and baling and no self respecting farmer would make hay on the Sabbath. Those who still had last years bales in the barn were feeling that they might be useful if the crop was ruined by wet weather.

This had been their life for generations. One year good, one year bad. Hence the saying, 'Make hay whilst the sun shines'. There was no time for lagging behind and this created a strong bond between neighbours. Probably your neighbours could be relatives, as before the days of motor transport all the young people did their courting within twelve miles of home resulting in a closed society. This formed a very small gene pool which increased the chances of breeding with distant relatives, producing many simpletons in the country areas.

Since the advent of motorised travel and as and our knowledge of breeding animals has developed, the picture in the countryside has changed dramatically and everyone is much more aware of the dangers of in-breeding and the advantages and hybrid vigour of the progeny when cross-breeding.

I was running the surgery on one such hot day. There were very few people in the waiting room and I noted a very large, fat lady with an equally obese dachshund. She had a bright, low-cut, floral summer dress, from which she was in grave danger of overflow. The holiday postcards with such ladies, the butt of seaside comedians, at once came to mind. Legs and thighs like tree trunks.

I waved goodbye to Marjorie Kewin whose dog I had just treated for that bane of summer months-fleas. "Don't forget to wash Timmy again in ten days time," I said to her as she departed.

The large floral lady got up with difficulty and waddled across the waiting room. "Mr Vetinry," I don't know what's to do with our Buster. Ever since we came over in the boat last week, all he's done is pant and scratch. There's summat serious up with 'im I think. It's not as if 'e eats a lot. Maybe it's 'is 'eart playin' up."

"We're staying in one of them boarding houses on't promenade. 'Pets welcome' they said, but after climbin' up three flights of stairs the poor little bugger's knackered. Mind you, the food's orl right and we can walk across the road and sit on the beach deckchairs, all day. Mind you you've got to be careful walkin' over in case you slip on the 'orse poo left behind by the trams. It's like crossin' no-man's land."

By this stage I was exhausted taking in all the information. "Excuse me madam, can you give me some details for my records in case I have to see your dog again. What is your name and where are you staying?"

"Maggie Haythornthwaite. We're stayin' at the Regal, and my dog is George, named after an old boy friend, who were a randy old sod. You won't believe it, but he hardly eats a thing. I don't know how he puts on so much weight. I think that Josie Allsopp, from next door, drops bread over the garden fence for him. You'd think that she'd 'ave more to do with her waste food. It could all be made into something nourishing for her husband, Bert, who looks like he might enter for the whippet racin'."

"Can I help you to lift him on the examination table Mrs Haythornthwaite."

"No! Best not to, 'as he can be a bit spiteful wi men." With one movement she grabbed hold of the hapless George, and as she lifted him onto the table he struggled, and in the next moment her low cut dress gave up the uneven struggle with her enormous bosom, which all flopped out on the table. I stood open mouthed, intrigued and wishing I was somewhere else. My first instinct was to lend a helping hand but instantly realised that this might not be appreciated. George looked indifferent and Maggie gave him a cuff across the ear. "Now yer' daft lummock. Look what yer' made me do." as she turned about and reinstalled her stately beauty.

She grabbed hold of George by the collar whilst I examined him carefully. "You seem to have a few problems here George. You have a heart murmur, and a nasty eczema caused by fleas. The fleas we can deal with by use of this powder, used as a wash every ten days, and use a block of sulphur in his drinking water to help the skin."

"The heart trouble is a bigger problem made worse by your excess weight. I think that you should go onto meat, with increasing amounts of chopped cabbage every day. He will eventually accept it. The cabbage will fill your tummy, and make you feel better, but it won't add to your weight. Cut right down on his biscuits! The other problems you have are the heat as your lungs are a bit congested, and having to climb up the stairs in the boarding house creates a problem in itself!"

"In many respects he would be better off staying in our kennels, whilst you and your husband enjoy your holiday. This will rest him and keep him out of the heat. You must take him to your vet when you go home, Mrs Haythornthwaite!"

We had many long discussions on the ethics of handling terminal disease cases in our patients, in contrast with our medical colleagues who, would chortle and say that we were lucky enough to be able to bury our mistakes.

It has always concerned me when my patients or my own animals aged and their vital functions such as kidneys, liver and heart start to fail. I recently had an old cat with dementia symptoms! These are often prolonged conditions where both owner and vet have time to consider the deterioration in the pet's health and formulate an approach to the situation. It is a different story when the presented condition is an emergency -

such as a tumour, thrombosis or a road traffic accident.

In all these cases we should consider the well being of the animal above all. After all our remit is to relieve suffering, whilst from a purely subjective viewpoint, this is a pet, devoted companion and also in many cases a child substitute. There is no magic formula, as dying is part of living. We become very emotional and selfish when initially faced with the possibility of parting with a loved one.

The veterinary surgeon is often thought of as being very cool when the final act of euthanasia takes place. We, and our nursing staff, could not function if we were involved in high emotion so we have to distance ourselves from the situation. Our first consideration is to ensure that euthanasia goes as smoothly as possible; our next thoughts are for the owners who are bereaved.

This simple act of dissociating oneself from euthanasia is a much discussed feature in the veterinary world, which has the highest suicide rate of all professions. Possibly when one is in a state of despair, and we see euthanasia as an everyday experience, the thought of suicide is not so frightening. Also we have the knowledge and the means!

We live in an age of advanced medical and surgical techniques and, despite all this knowledge we are still very confused about the way we should proceed. Modern medicine is inclined to maintain life against all odds, as we have the belief that life is a sacred gift. Unfortunately this can so easily put the patient through months of pain, undignified procedures and expense until inevitably death, which is inevitable, supervenes.

Our colleagues in the medical profession were often castigated publicly, and struck off the medical register for assisting patients, often in extreme pain, to die in peace by the excessive use of pain relievers such as morphine or barbiturates. This to me is true compassion as their remit is also to relieve suffering..

I feel that this was more widespread and overlooked by previous generations when many drugs were unavailable. Indeed I recall in the days of the notorious Dr Bodkin Adams, a doctor on trial for patient euthanasia, seeing my father a very caring and compassionate family practitioner, being quizzed by my brother, a medical student. "Dad, have you ever helped a patient to die?"

With the wisdom of age he turned and replied quietly, "You must learn to mind your own business!" I am sure that this does occur with those doctors who care for their patients comfort above all but it is only discussed between physician and patient.

From a purely veterinary viewpoint I have always discussed the animal having a poor prognosis with the owners.

Their first reaction is often very personal. "Expense is no object. We must care for him until he dies" Often I might reply, "If he were my pet I would realise that he is now at the point of no return but the final decision is yours. All that is ahead of him is a continual deterioration in his well-being and enjoyment of life. He has given you a lifetime of devotion. You must decide what is fair."

I had the misfortune to sprain my wrist when a husky young steer crashed me into a gate so I ended up wearing a sling for a few days. I had never managed to be chauffeur-driven before but Mary gallantly offered to look after me. As we drew away from the surgery, she said, "your legs are alright aren't they, after your steer wrestling?"

"Yes!" I replied, somewhat perplexed by her direct approach. "Why do you ask? It's unlike you to be so caring!"

"You just sit in the passenger's seat. I'm captain of this ship and I don't want any winding up or leg-pulling." Rather bemused and affronted that I should stir things up I relied lamely. "Why?"

"Because I'm the captain, and any mutinous behaviour means that you walk the plank, or get out and walk back home!"

Least said was soonest mended! At our first call she treated some lame sheep without me advising her how to do the job. The second visit was minor surgery on a cow's damaged teat where I kept my counsel and congratulated her on a job well done.

Our final call before lunch was to Dave Quilleash at Ballelby to castrate a litter of piglets. He had meticulously cleaned out the feed pen for our work and said "I'll just go and get you a bale of straw to put your gear on. He disappeared in the direction of the haggard (stack yard) where he had the bales stacked.

"I'll go into the pen and drive out the piglets," I said feeling useless. "Oh no, you won't. You're an invalid and might need both hands. Leave this to me!" With that comment she leapt over the wall just as Dave returned. Standing at the low entrance with the flap half lifted she turned towards us. There was a loud squeal as Blodwen, the sow, shot out between her legs, carrying Mary on her back across the pen, both hands gripping tight onto the sow's ears in true jockey style. Blodwen stopped suddenly, and Mary was dumped at the first fence into the trough full of pig swill. She stood up, a sorry sight, dripping and unhappy whilst Dave and I leant over the wall convulsed in laughter and wishing that we had a camera.

"Stay there, Miss!" chortled Dave, "I'll just get a pail of warm water and a towel to rub you down, lest you smell the house out! Then inside for a cup of tea to settle you down."

Humility is hard to bear but Mary accepted her role heroically. I did offer to drive her back to the surgery, but was instantly rebuffed and ordered to sit still and buy the drinks when we got home.

Stories abound in the realms of veterinary folklore. None of us are immune and indeed these anecdotes have entertained many after dinner stories. One which I shall never forget took place shortly after Mary's sow riding episode.

It was a lovely morning in late spring, when all was well with the world. Revelling in such a beautiful day, I completely forgot Gilhooly's law which clearly states that some of one's most embarrassing or frightening situations in life can recur, in different guises. Possibly it is the Great Creator cutting us down to size when we have forgotten incidents such as 'Annie' the enraged sow, belonging to Finbar Rafferty, who held me imprisoned in the hay rack until help appeared!

Moira and I had for some time been concerned about Brian's love life which to the idle bystander appeared to have gone quiet. In reality it had become an in-house affair as both he and Mary seemed to be spending a lot of time practicing for her appearance at the Southern Show later in the year. It was evident in their body language and there was a lot of playful ribbing between them. Que sera sera!

It was a car washing morning when Ruth interrupted my chores and called out "Ned! Can you come and speak to Mr Quilleash, Ballaragh farm. He's got a heifer that has gone mad!" Dropping everything I rushed in to the phone. "Hello Dave. What's the problem today?"

His voice was tense with suppressed anxiety. "Ned! Do you remember that we had a case of bracken poisoning on the hill last year. It looks as if we have another. You did say that they would sometimes bleed at the nose and go a bit aggressive. This looks like one. She had a go at me up on the hill and fortunately 'Nell' the cattle dog drove her off. We've just got her into the yard with the help of a few neighbours, and chased her into a loosebox. Can you get out fairly soon or someone might be hurt."

Turning to Mary I said, "Have you seen many bracken poisoning cases or is the land in Yorkshire too poor to support it?

She flushed and retorted tartly, "you watch it young man or you might become severely damaged. The land in Yorkshire is too rich for bracken, but as I have never seen a case I am prepared to come and advise you on treatment. So let's go!"

She had acquired a pretty little Morris 1000 to replace her battered old Hillman, so we opted to go in my Hillman as the roads on the hill could be fairly rough. As we drove out towards Laxey, Mary muttered tentatively, "Tell me honestly Ned, have you ever seen a case of bracken poisoning before or is this all blarney?

Looking straight ahead, I responded trying to suppress a smile, "Really Mary! I am surprised at you disbelieving me. I can understand a Liverpool graduate not having my vast experience. You see, in the west of Ireland, bracken is almost a garden plant. The dried form has been used for many years as bedding for the livestock because hay and straw are too valuable a crop and kept for fodder. The cattle don't particularly like it, but in the springtime when grass is short they graze the pasture closely and eat the early shoots. This can take up to two months to show symptoms of disease, which is anaemia and muscle haemorrhage. I have seen violent bloody diarrhoea with bleeding from nostrils and eyes. Sometimes there is a mental reaction when they become very aggressive and dangerous."

"Really, said Mary, "As we had very little plant toxicology at college. I've learnt a lot."

"We were exceptionally lucky as our toxicology lecturer would bring the plant into lectures and describe cases he had seen. It all came alive. I saw one case, last year on the farm, which died and of course there is no effective cure. The case I saw at Dave's last year was a yearling which was dying. Let's see what he's got today!"

We drove along the road in comparative silence, which was strange as we normally chattered constantly. Almost naively, I commented, "Tell me Mary? I'm a little concerned because you have been very quiet lately. Is it problems with Tom or are you not enjoying practice as much as you hoped?"

I didn't have to glance sideways to be aware that she was blushing deeply and rather uneasy. "No Ned, Tom and I are only good friends and I'm perfectly happy in the practice. The trouble with you Manxmen is that the slightest gossip becomes reality!" It was almost like Brian speaking.

Having confirmed my suspicions, I retracted saying, "Sorry old thing but, as we have known each other for many years, I was a bit concerned and you realise that on the Island everyone knows your business before you do." She laid a hand on mine and apologised. "Sorry Ned, I just have a couple of worries on my mind!"

In Laxey we turned off the steep hill towards Ballaragh, and very soon turned in to the yard entrance. Like so many hillside farms on the Island, the buildings were built in a square to protect stock and workers from the elements. In the centre was a pit where all the straw and dung from the sheds were pitch forked out each day before being spread on the fields. These dung heaps were a haven for flies in the summer and a happy hunting ground for the fat chickens, who scratched along the surface all day in pursuit of succulent morsels, accompanied by a contented krrk-krrk of happiness.

Dave was in the yard to meet us. "Sorry to be such a fusspot, Ned. I didn't want anyone hurt and know that you are used to dealin' with these situations!"

"Dave!" I said, looking over the top of the dung pile to the cowshed. "The noise coming out of the shippon makes me wonder whether there will be anything left when she's finished!"

"She's in the old calving box at the end, yessir! Although I'm having doubts about its strength."

"Have you met Mary Sutherland, our new colleague, who has come along to assist? She's a smart hand at calvings if you're ever in trouble. I would suggest that I walk along the side of the dung heap and open the door, if you two come behind me with a pitchfork in case we have problems."

How could I tell him that I was terrified of the situation, as he had such trust in me. Gingerly I unlatched the door and stepped inside. The once pretty, in-calf Ayrshire heifer had made short work of the upright slats surrounding the loosebox. She was very agitated, with bloody saliva surrounding her mouth and one look at me and the day-lit entrance triggered her off to try to climb the partition. The aged timbers crumbled and as she staggered to her feet I recalled the adage 'Those that turn and run away,live to fight another day! With a bellow she charged down the shed as I shot out the door and started climbing the dung pile. The further I ascended the deeper I sank in the rich heap, almost feeling the heifers breath on my neck. 'Please God! What do I do now?' As my hands clawed at the dung mountain ahead.

Suddenly I realised that I was on my own, and, looking back saw that the heifer, with her beautifully curved horns, had tried to follow. My prayer was answered as her small feet and extra weight plunged her deep into the pile, and stopped her instantly.

Dave and Mary looked on in horror and relief at my narrow escape. "Mary!" I cried. "Get the long rope from the car. Dave I feel that you should call the slaughterman to shoot the poor beast!"

Dave stood guard with the pitchfork but 'Blossom' the heifer was going nowhere. Her exertions only served to exhaust her. Within a couple of minutes, Mary returned with the rope announcing, "Don't bother about the phone, Dave. Your wife has kindly offered to contact the slaughterman"

Dave laid a large loop of rope around the haft of the pitchfork and dropped it over the heifer's horns. He took the other end of the rope and fastened it firmly around the 'stiddle' to which the cows' neck chain was fastened. "That should keep her under control and her head is pulled round sideways!"

After a few minutes a peremptory toot on a car horn heralded the arrival of the slaughterman, and the round and jolly form of Jim Caley walked into the yard with a captive bolt pistol in his hand. "Nice to see you've got her well restrained, Dave, I wasn't lookin' forward to this. At least her head's facin' towards me. Maybe this young lady would like to help Ned off the dung heap! I can't imagine what he's doing up there! Likely tryin' to catch some of your old scratchin' chickens" he finished, chuckling loudly.

He walked up to the heifer, loaded the pistol and carefully placed it at the exact spot on Blossom's skull before pulling the trigger. She dropped instantly, all her suffering at an end! That is the skill of the professional slaughterman!

Margaret Quilleash could not have been more concerned when I entered her house stinking of cow dung and my trousers and shirt covered with well rotted manure. She immediately sent Dave upstairs to bring down trousers and a shirt while she prepared a pot of tea with cupcakes. "My dear Ned, you go out the back and put on these clothes and put your own into this old grain sack. You all deserve a cuppa tea. It's sad to lose Blossom but there was nothin' else that we could do!

I returned to the kitchen amidst much laughter as Dave's trousers were four inches too short and his shirt a bit tight. Mary, with tears streaming down her face said, "Ned, you should enter into the Pierrot show on the promenade. I'm sure that the customers in the Jolly Farmer will have heard about your fancy dress by nightfall!"

As we left the farm I commented, "Mary, as a student, did you ever visit the farm up above here on the hillside, belonging to George Hanson?"

There was a short pause as she smiled. "Yes Ned! If I'm not mistaken wasn't that a training ground to test out students for speed and agility? I recall going up there with Brian a couple of times to attend a Galloway cow, flat out on the hillside with grass tetany. Correct me if I'm wrong, but at stage one, we would stagger up the hill to the cow which was struggling on the ground. The student was instructed to sit on the patient's head lest she struggled and hurt herself. Brian would slowly inject calcium and magnesium into the vein whilst Mr Hanson would gaze dreamily across the sea at Cumberland saying, "That's where I want my ashes scattered when the great call comes, Mr Vet. I chased scores of young girls across those fells in my day!"

"Then would start stage two, when I was directed to remain seated on the cow's head whilst farmer and vet walked down the field with all the gear and through the gate to safety."

"At stage three I would be directed to pull the cow to sitting up, and hurry along to join them lest the patient might be aggressive. At that juncture the cow would see a fuzzy figure and realise that this could be a threat to her darling calf. With a bellow, she would set off in pursuit. Of course by this time I was running headlong towards the wall and gate with an angry mummy, who could kill me, in full flight and rapidly catching up. I would collapse at the feet of George and Brian who were taking bets as to whether I would make it!"

I stopped the car to wipe my eyes. "Funny old thing but Brian never did tell me that you were trained there. The last time I ran down that hill I stumbled in a pot hole and fell over the wall. Mummy cow was so vexed and close behind me that she hit the gate and ran off down the field with a five bar gate as a necklet I think that we should return home now and I can put my clothes in the wash yet again! Of course tomorrow you are off to the show. Enjoy it and return with lots of jumping rosettes. I shall try to call in for a few minutes."

I dropped Mary off at the surgery and didn't stay long as Brian and Ruth were enjoying my 'borrowed clothes' to the full and I was sent off to change as we were going out to dinner that evening. At least my story added to the evening's entertainment.

The following morning was bright and sunny and the air full of birdsong After a long spell of warm weather some of the birds were sitting on their third clutch of eggs! All was well with the world.

It looked as if all the world were heading to the Southern Show. My only call was to see a lame pony.

The first person to enter the surgery was a timid little lady who crept in like a little mouse. "Er, Good morning Mr Carson. I was sent in to you by Mr Jack Quayle, the owner of 'Mouse' whose life you saved last year. My name is Brenda Pascoe"

We're at our wit's end. A few months ago we were given a little Basenji dog. You'll know the yodelling dog from the Belgian Congo. He is such a pretty animal with a lovely curled tail, but of late he seems to have taken a dislike to my husband. My husband is a postman and has to work very hard. Every evening when he comes home, the dog is in my husband's favourite chair by the fire. When he tries to move 'Rupert', the dog, he immediately growls and has several times attacked him. Now we are both afraid of him, and he has started cocking his leg on the furniture. The smell is awful and we just don't know what to do. He is often very affectionate and loves being stroked and cuddled, but is also so unpredictable. Do you think that he's ill or in pain?"

I have never been good at long distance diagnosis. "Why don't you bring him in, so that I can see him?"

"Oh that's easy", responded Mrs Pascoe. "Ryan is sitting out in the garden with him" and off she trotted to return in two minutes with Ryan and Rupert. I have always regarded the Basenji as a most delightful dog to look at. With a golden tan and white coat, prick ears and a very alert look and curly tail they draw one's attention at once.

Ryan was even smaller than his wife and Rupert was not a very happy dog. He presented his flank to me in a 'don't touch' I'm in charge attitude.

"Can you lift him on the table for examination?" I commenced. "Both of the Pascoes responded. "He's in one of his moods and might well bite us."

"Alright," I replied. I took the end of his lead so that his head was stretched up in the air, and he couldn't bite, and with my hand under his chest, I quickly lifted him onto the examination table. Keeping the leash stretched I gently smoothed him down talking quietly. He accepted this change and gently relaxed and I was able to examine him.

Turning to the astonished owners I continued "Look! He is in a strange situation and I have asserted my authority which he has accepted. Are you firm with him at home, Ryan, or do you back down to him when he growls?"

"We don't want to upset him so we leave him alone until he moves away."

"Who feeds Rupert?"

"Well I do generally!" replied Brenda before I take him for a walk. He's as good as gold wi' me!"

I pondered for a minute. "I think that the problem is in the relationship that Rupert has with Ryan. A dog is a pack animal, and there has to be a pack leader and he realises that Ryan is the other male in the house. This business of jumping up on your lap when he wishes, makes him feel that he is the pack leader, and he must control his pack-that's you! It's his instinct and if there is no other leader he will fill that position. This is why he is cocking his leg on the furniture as a territory-marking process! A good wash down with strong disinfectant should remove his odour."

"You must reverse the situation, and become the alpha male in the pack. Ryan must feed him and take him on walks. In this manner he relies on you for his creature comforts and will be subservient to you. Teach him that his place is on the floor. Physical domination is unnecessary. The tone of your voice is all it requires. In the wild there is no such thing as 'rights'. All members follow instructions and if they don't do so they may be killed or exiled by the alpha male or female. The female wolf growls at her pups and gets obedience. I train my own dogs to realise that if I growl they are in trouble. We live in a permissive society which accounts for the bad behaviour of some of our young people. Go home and try his new regime and come back and see me in two weeks"

All stories should have a happy ending In this case Ryan called me in a fortnight to say the transformation in Rupert was remarkable. Once the dog realised that he must not bite the hand that feeds him he changed his allegiance to Ryan who had become the alpha male. Ryan in his turn gained confidence and started training him so that he became a pleasure to handle.

As I drove southwards towards the Southern show, I had reason to think upon the recent events. People were becoming much more involved emotionally with their pets and yet they understood them less as animals that worked! We were increasingly having problems with pedigree animals being bred too closely for show purposes, until they were a travesty of the original animal. Hunting dogs such as borzois and smooth fox terriers were being bred with narrower heads resulting in less brain capacity-they were designer dogs! Cocker spaniels were also highly strung and even pekinese had developed an aggressive streak. No wonder that Maxwell Knight, in his book 'Animals and Ourselves,' commented that he was tempted to entitle it 'Save Us From Our Friends'

Man and Beast

When pedigree animals are but a travesty of the original working breed, it makes a mockery of the original breed merely to satisfy the whims of mankind.

I arrived at the show ground as the horses were being exercised in the warming-up area. Most of the contestants I knew quite well and the normally cheerful riders were now channelled in their efforts to attain the winners accolade. Brian was standing at the ringside watching Mary riding 'Jade' who had been jumping flawlessly and had already qualified for the final jump-offs. Jade was distracted and knocked one of the bars and immediately started carrying her foreleg in pain. Mary slid out of the saddle to check the problem. As she bent forward and lifted Jade's foot, a young girl rode past on her feisty little pony. Mary moved and the pony, spooked by the movement, lashed out with her hindleg, catching her on the head with her hoof.

Mary dropped – pole-axed! A gasp of horror arose from the spectators. In the following seconds the St John's First Aiders grabbed their gear but not before Brian rushed forward and cradled Mary's inert form in his arms.

He was gently pushed aside by the first aid team and a doctor acquaintance, Neville, from amongst the spectators. He was the picture of dejection as he stood back so I took him by the arm saying, "Brian! There is nothing we can do at

192

the moment so let's have a cup of tea until we can speak to the doctor in a couple of minutes."

We sat in the refreshment tent listening to the concerned comments of our friends. He sat looking into space, tears in his eyes, muttering "Why didn't I get out there and examine the mare. Thank God that we bought her a new strengthened riding hat last week. What would I do without her?"

At that moment the doctor appeared and sat down at the table. "She's a lucky young lady Brian! Quite concussed but otherwise no damage! We are sending her off to Noble's hospital for x-ray as a precaution! You will probably be able to see her this evening. Sister Reid is on duty and will look after you"

By the time that I had finished surgery in the evening, Brian had returned from the hospital to announce that Mary was sitting up in bed and feeling much better. I called to see her on the way home. I was ushered in by the sister. "Don't be getting her too excited now. I know you of old!" she warned me, smiling.

Mary was lying in the bed, head swathed in bandages. She smiled as I took her hand, saying, "Mary, I don't think that I've ever seen you look quite so entrancing. Rather like an animated mummy! How are you feeling?"

She giggled, replying "I've never felt better thank you!" and, with a grimace, "apart from a splitting headache. Did I collapse gracefully? How is the poor girl whose pony walloped me?"

Surprised, I replied. "What do you mean, you never felt better? First of all you stood in the wrong position, and lost your chance for the B.S.J.A. trophy. Not only that, you might have been killed!"

"My dear Ned! He did it at last! Brian was so upset that he sent the sister out and then he proposed to me. I guessed that it would happen soon, but he was almost in tears at the thought of losing me. I'm slightly concussed, but flying on a cloud!"

"Thank goodness for that. Moira and I were going to have to speak to him strongly. The drums have been beating all over the Island for weeks. When I phoned through to Brian the other evening, the telephone operator, John Kewin, told me that Brian had taken you out to the Fort Anne for a romantic dinner. He finished off by commenting 'She'll make an honest man of him yet!' We can only say that we are both delighted to share in your happiness and now you will be making plans"

"Yes Ned! We must be thanking you both for being such good friends to us. I've got such a headache so you may kiss my hand. Goodnight!"

I said farewell and headed home to bring the good tidings to Moira. It was an exciting evening for us both, as the whole situation in the Island would change.

The engagement news spread like wildfire. The eligible bachelor and attractive young vet were part of the Manx society and the inevitable chaos of organising dates, venues and guests kept the couple very occupied. Fortunately, I was excluded, although Moira was called in on an advisory basis. Eventually Easter was chosen as the best time, and the service was to be at St Georges Church with the reception at the Castle Mona Hotel.

It looked very much as if my aspirations in the Island would not come to fruition, as the practice could not sustain three partners!

In the army every private aims to become a sergeant, and my aim was to own a practice! I was torn between either staying in my Celtic homeland, or following my ambition as a vet and running my own practice.

After much discussion between Moira and me, we decided after talking to Brian and Mary, that I must search for a suitable mixed practice but where do we go!

There were many vacancies across the British Isles, but I had always been associated with country areas, and I felt comfortable with my Celtic connections where we were far away from big cities and over-large farms. I saw many jobs advertised in lucrative small animal practices, particularly in the home counties, but I could not have fitted in with a clientele whose sense of values regarding their animals differed so much from mine. Scotland and Wales were attractive, but we were drawn to the magic that we had experienced on our honeymoon in Cornwall. There were several vacancies in Devon, but the advert that attracted us was in a practice on the edge of Dartmoor, which was primarily cattle and sheep work.

Moira suggested that I apply for the post so after a word with Brian and Mary I wrote away for details of the practice. Several days later Moira called me in from the garden to say that there was a Scotsman on the phone in reply to my job application. I gathered myself together, suddenly very nervous. "Good evening, Ned Carson here. My wife tells me that you are calling about my job application!"

"Good evening laddie." came the terse response. "Campbell McKellar speaking. We were very interested in your application. Tell me a bit more about your experience. We have a five-man practice here, mainly involved in cattle and sheep. Quite a bit of dairy work, and a few horses. The work is rough and ready on the moor, and we would give a good return for your labours. Most of our clients are on family farms. Nothing fancy mind you but they seem to appreciate our help. We have a lot of lambing during the springtime and also quite a bit of redwater in the cattle. Have you had much experience of giving blood transfusions? There are also quite a few caesareans in the South Devon cattle which we expect everyone to get involved in"

Rather taken aback by all this information I replied weakly. "Well 'er yes we have some redwater in the Island, and I have carried out several caesareans, but as yet, I've not been involved in blood transfusions, although I'm keen to learn any new skills. Do you have a small animal surgery, as I have done quite a bit of work on that aspect. We have two young children and hope to start them in school in the future."

"In that case laddie, why don't you come down and see us. We are a progressive practice and reward industry. We shall pay your expenses. Bring your wife, as you no doubt realise they are invaluable members of the practice and should also be able to fit in. We do have radio telephones in the cars, which saves a lot of doubling back on your tracks. Although the hours can sometimes be long we all work together as a team!

The river Tavy runs through the town and we are fairly near to Exeter and Plymouth and of course there are miles of moorland close by for the children to adventure. If you and your wife like the idea give me a ring during the next few days as we are quite short staffed."

I put down the phone, did a little jig and picked Moira up in my arms, saying, "He appeared quite interested, and has asked us down to see the practice. Would you be happy in the West Country?"

Supportive as ever Moira smiled happily. "If this is going to make you happy, I'm sure that we can make a go of it, love!"

I arrived at the surgery early next morning to pass on the good news. Bryan was delighted that we were being so positive. "I'm sure this chap will ring me for a reference. I'll back you up to the hilt!" Mary was much quieter and sad "Ned, we've been good friends for a long time and now I feel that you have to leave because of me, and depart from your homeland, where you are so well thought of."

"Don't worry about us, Mary. I think that Ronnie Kaighin up in Cronk y Voddy will comfort you when you appear with a fishing rod! There's a big world out there with lots of new challenges and experiences. Anyway, Moira has quite set her mind on the idea." Whimsically I commented. "Of course you could break off the engagement and stay as an assistant!"

"Ned Carson! She retorted in that steely tone which inferred trouble. "If I didn't like you so much I could strangle you but you will have to be here until after the wedding—please!"

"Brian, I said, "we should go and attend this interview fairly soon in order to make a decision about a move. We shan't be available to join them until after the wedding, so it will mean that we would start in the spring as Easter is early. Would it suit you both if we head off to Devon at the beginning of October? If all goes well and we join this practice, it will give us lots of time to organise your nuptials."

"You are free to go, when you please Ned! We shall fit in around you and I have forbidden Mary to take any more part in horse sports in the meantime, "Although," he added mischievously, "a good bang on the head seems to have knocked some sense into her!"

"That's it, I've had enough," interjected Mary, stamping her foot, as we chortled like a pair of schoolboys, "I'm off to plight my troth with Ronnie Kaighin!"

It took several days to settle the travel arrangements for our trip to Devon. Fortunately Moira's sister was happy to look after the children for a few days in Wigan, whilst we headed off to our interview. To avoid arriving looking too travel worn, we decided to drive via Exmoor and stay overnight at Lynmouth. We enjoyed our visit, to this pretty little town, which was tinged with sadness at the problems that they had suffered in the catastrophic flooding several years before, when many people died as swollen rivers torrented through the town.

The next morning broke with wall-to-wall sunshine and, as we headed towards Exeter, we enjoyed views across the wild moorland country with sheep and cattle scattered across the rough terrain. We became quite excited at the prospect of Dartmoor, after seeing the beauty of the

Exmoor countryside, with its secluded farmsteads and villages scattered randomly.

We made the decision to drive through Exeter and Ashburton, and head across the moor in order to see the area covered by the practice, including Princetown with its notorious prison. The moor was in one of its dour moods with thick cloud hanging across the hills, and our introduction to the prison was below lowering skies, with patches of mist obscuring the distant tors.

A quick glance at the road map told us that we would rapidly drop down from Pork Hill to Tavistock and the valley of the River Tavy. We were soon to see Pork Hill with its regular rainfall, ever welcoming visitors to the Tavy valley. It is on these slopes that rain clouds driven by the prevailing south westerlies dump much of their moisture as they hit the sharp uplift towards Princetown.

Despite our sadness at leaving our Island, Moira was overwhelmed with the scenic beauty of the moor, particularly as the sun lit up the hills and she chattered happily. "Look at the views dear. I'm itching to paint some of the scenery!"

Suddenly, we were down into the town and, carefully following our instructions, drove into the square where we parked and sought some lunch. A short walk up the riverside and we sat down to a very pleasant snack in Goode's café.

It was still early for our interview so we had a wee walk through the town to savour the atmosphere. None of the big chain stores to be seen. A delicatessen, shoe shop and a store selling newspapers all took our interest. Moira laid her hand on my arm, "Look at the beautiful church. Let's take a look inside, and then have a wander through the pannier market. The whole of the centre is so picturesque"

After a few minutes we followed directions out along the Whitchurch Road until we found the address and turned in at "Greystones". A short way up the drive a solid victorian family house came into view, with much of the façade covered by a magnificent wisteria. The front door bell shrilled and, amidst much shouting in the background Anne MacKellar appeared, smiling broadly. She had a radiant face which exuded friendliness.

"Hello! You must be Ned and Moira. Welcome to Tavistock. I'm Anne, Campbell has just gone out on a call but should be back soon. You must be tired from travelling. I've just put the kettle on for a cup of tea, so do join me." A crash sounded from upstairs and turning to face the hallway she said, "Sorry, discipline problems!" and in a voice befitting a regimental sergeant major she bellowed, "Will you children get your rooms tidied up at once. I shall be up to check in ten minutes, and woe betide you if they're not shipshape!"

Smiling, she added. "Don't have four boys unless you relish a running battle with discipline. Come into the kitchen and we can talk, whilst I'm making tea. Don't trip over the toolbox. Its mine, I've just been repairing this electric socket. I'm odd job man, cook, disciplinarian and telephone answering service. His lordship is too busy on practice matters and intellectual pursuits.

Tell me about yourselves. How many children have you? What are your interests, veterinary and family wise? Campbell never tells me the interesting nitty gritty bits. He's all business talk. You must have said some of the right things when you talked to him, as he generally likes to check references."

Anne struck us as rather reserved but extremely friendly. Half way through our chat there was crackling and a voice in the front hall. "Excuse me! That's the 'Lord and Master' calling on the radio telephone." She returned after a couple of minutes. "He'll be with us in a couple of minutes, after he's bought his Woodbines. He's an addict to work and tobacco."

There was a scrunching of tyres on the driveway as the Austin Westminster drew up outside the front door and Campbell strode in. He was nearly six feet tall, thickset build with a ruddy complexion, an ideal build in a rugby scrum! He had an inexpressive mouth of the type that does not smile readily and blue grey eyes staring out from steel rimmed spectacles. I at once had an impression that he was a man of power and intent. He brought to mind the title of a book I was reading, "Fame is the Spur" by Howard Spring. He was a man driven by success"

He was courtesy itself with smiles and solicitous attention to Moira. "Did you have a good trip? It's a long, tiring journey from Liverpool. Did you stay overnight on the way down? Whilst we are having tea, tell me more about yourselves."

"Moira, you have been married some years now. How much have you been involved in the practice as we value our wives to the extent that they are involved as a telephone answering service and must be paid appropriately? At present we have five members, and one has just moved on, and another is looking into a practice opportunity. The larger a practice grows the more the presence of responsible partners is required for administration to maintain a stable service to our clients."

"Yes!" responded Moira, not knowing what to make of this unusual man. "I agree with you but we must not lose sight of the fact that we have a duty to our children also and if we organise our lives correctly this should be no problem!" There was a momentary pause as Anne said "Hmm" and Campbell continued, "I can see that we shall get on well lassie! You seem to have your values balanced.

"I think that Anne has arranged a meal at Two Bridges for us this evening and we have reserved a room for you at the Queen's Hotel tonight. May I take you for a short tour of the area and you can see the territory in which we work? I'll give you a map to follow our progress. We have every client included in a map reference book so that newcomers don't get lost."

He ushered us out to the car and as we drove off he remarked, "this is the Plymouth road where we have quite a number of clients. The next town is Yelverton where we have a number of clients, mostly equine. Have you done much horse work Ned?"

I enjoy working with horses but I can't claim to be an expert!" I responded, although we do not have a hunt in the Island.

"Don't worry laddie." Up around Yelverton we have some of the pseudo-county set who talk the lingo but don't know much about horses but on the other hand we have many experienced horse people. Did you go through National Service?"

"Yes" I said. "most of my time was spent in the Veterinary Corps at Melton Mowbray. I enjoyed life in the horse lines until a rather smart adjutant decided that I would be well employed as an office clerk. That is when I fell out of love with the army and had to satisfy myself riding the colonel's horse bareback around the fields at midnight! My other outstanding accomplishment was to be appointed latrine orderly for a week!"

As we drove through the town, we veered off onto the Princetown road and up onto the wild moorland. Bracken was everywhere, interspersed with gorse and patches of grass well nibbled by scores of Black faced sheep, Galloway cattle and Dartmoor ponies. There was an immense sense of freedom, with the horizon consisting of rocky tors and stone walls, winding across the landscape. Small twisted thorn bushes, reflecting the poor quality of the soil leaned over sideways in obeisance to the prevailing wind. I felt the same sense of excitement which always stimulated me as I drove over the top of the Isle of Man.

Suddenly we were in Princetown and skirting Dartmoor prison, that grim and grey monolith built to house the French prisoners in the Napoleonic Wars and then conscientious objectors during the first world war. Since that time it has served various functions.

"We do quite a lot of work on the prison farm," commented Campbell, "there is a dairy herd, pig farm and a lot of beef cattle on the moors. We always keep our cars locked, as they are pretty quick off the mark if you leave them for a couple of minutes! As time is getting on I think that we should take you back to the hotel in order to rest and change and pick you up about 7.30 for a meal. I shall let you see our premises which we are planning to develop as there are virtually no small animal facilities and we operate from a small office and garage."

"Here we are laddie!" We turned into a narrow alleyway with a couple of matt brown doors and a cobwebbed window. As he got out he beckoned to Moira and me to follow through the small open door leading into a room with bare worn floorboards, lined with shelves supported dozens of Winchester bottles containing chloroform, ether, Fowlers solution and many other pharmaceutical preparations. None of the branded medicines sold by the modern drug companies were evident.

In a small side room stood a tiny bespectacled little man with a cap from a previous era. "William, meet Mr and Mrs Carson who may be joining us." William touched his cap to Moira, shook my hand and said, in a deep voice, which belied his size. "Very pleased to meet you. I hope that you enjoy Tavistock, sir"

"William," continued Campbell smiling, "has been with the firm for many years, initially as coachmen to Mr Fraser, my predecessor, and he now works in the surgery as receptionist and dispenser. What William doesn't know about dispensing isn't worth knowing, is it William?" "No Mr MacKellar, sir", responded William, tipping his cap once more.

"Come and see the drug store next door, and follow me" as we stepped out into the lane and he slid back a large double door leading into what must have once been the stables. There were more rows of shelving containing proprietary drugs, mysterious brown boxes, and 40 gallon barrels full of Epsom salts, treacle, copper sulphate and nux vomica (a strychnine based powder). This is our basic dispensary, where William is in charge and woe betide anyone who makes a mess in here.

I don't know how interested you are, Moira, but we should have a look in the garage at the back which fits as lambing shed and operating theatre." Campbell led us into an empty garage, with a kitchen cabinet on one side and a sturdy operating table with a wooden top fitted with numerous key holes to assist in tying down sheep for surgery.

"We generally have one man in the surgery all day from 15th February for six weeks doing nothing but lambings and sheep caesareans. It is an exhausting period, and as you can see, rather cold in this garage when there is snow on the ground!"

At that moment a very dirty Wolsley screeched around the corner and pulled up in front of the office. Out jumped a tall, dark man with glasses. "Do you want a job Campbell? I'm just meeting David and we're off to a blood transfusion in Peter Tavy."

"No thanks George," was the response. "Come and meet my friends. This is Moira and Ned Carson from the Isle of Man. They've come over to see what we are like, as Ned may replace Ken Blake when he leaves!"

Turning to us he continued, "meet George Carter, our senior vet, who tries to keep us organised. We carry out many blood transfusions every year and save a lot of lives in severe redwater cases. The disease can be very acute here. Seen in the morning and dead by evening"

"Greetings!" said George. "Have you had much redwater in your practice?

"I've only seen two cases in two years so I can see that I shall have to brush up my diagnosis! I replied.

"Nice to meet you. Sorry if it's brief but I must gather up the transfusion gear and meet David on the farm."

"Before we go" said Campbell, "let me take you to the small animal department. This has to be the worst room that you have ever seen, but it's rented and not worth spending money on." He opened a little door and we entered a tiny room, about six feet by six feet with cobwebs over the windows and the walls covered with peeling whitewash. "I'm not proud of it, but I also have ideas for the future"

Campbell took us home so that we could collect the car and return to the hotel, promising to collect us at seven o'clock. As we changed, Moira asked, "what are your first impressions?"

"Mixed!" was my immediate response. "What a tremendous place to get experience, new skills which I may never have acquired in the Island. He is a dominant and creative character full of ideas and drive. It would never be smooth sailing, as it is with Brian. I am quite excited at the opportunity in such a gorgeous area, and the sea is only 20 miles away. Positive vibes so far"

On time, we met the McKellars at the door and were whisked away in the Westminster. "We are off to eat at the Two Bridges Hotel, just past the prison," commented Campbell." Anne interrupted, saying, "You could have stayed with us and eaten at home but I would not recommend it. Four noisy and irrepressible young boys would be a constant interruption."

"Tell me about yourself Moira. What did you do before you met Ned and what are your interests? All people coming for interview are quizzed in this manner to see if you can settle in our little town."

"I am a physical education teacher and have been teaching for about seven years. As for my interests, I love art and crafts and enjoy gardening and looking after the children- Donal is four and Alison just over two years of age. We both enjoy the outdoors and swimming."

"Here we are," announced Campbell, as we pulled up to the door of the hotel. "Everything at your service, a comfortable hotel, fishing in the river Dart and walking as far as the eye can see. Let's go in and announce our presence. Moira, what would you care to drink? Anne is a G&T and Ned I should imagine that you might enjoy a pint."

Drinks ordered we wandered into the dining room and were ushered to our table to study the menu and chat. "Campbell," I commenced, "I'm not used to this business of interviews. Can you tell me what you want in an assistant, and I can reply from there?"

"Well laddie" he preambled, "I am looking for a colleague who is not afraid of work, gets on with the local farmers and is prepared to knuckle down to a challenge. We all share work equally although I must confess some of mine is administration, which would appear that I don't always carry the labour part."

"You would be paid your membership of veterinary associations. Initiative and willingness to research into disease conditions is good for the soul. The firm will supply house and car and send you off on courses every year as knowledge is continually improving. The world is what you make it!

Let's sample these lovely steaks!" he said, "and we shall chat over the meal!" Several times during the meal other customers greeted Anne or himself, which I felt was a good omen as they evidently socialised and had many contacts.

The sweet course was over and we sat enjoying our coffee. "Campbell, I am interested in what we have seen and heard so far. I really enjoy farmers and farm work and listening to you earlier about developing the small animal side also makes me excited. I presume that there is room for expansion if the small animal side is encouraged. What long-term prospects are there for assistants in the practice?"

"My rugger days are past but I enjoy the company of friends in the Round Table. It gives fellowship and a social life for both of us and at the same time, we take part in worthwhile charities."

"It's about time we headed homewards and we can discuss the practice on the way. We all will do some of the horse work, although because I have a hunter and Point-to-Point on occasion I will be lumbered with much of it. There was another colleague, called Malseed, when I arrived and we could not see eye-to-eye so I quickly got rid of him. He was a good practitioner but we had a different vision. As you have spoken in a forthright manner I'm sure that we could get on together. How much salary would you be wanting?"

Taken off guard I thought rapidly. It must better my current salary of £1100 pounds! "How about twelve hundred pounds?" I commented with all the confidence of a three-year graduate

Silence ensued as Campbell mulled over my comment. Without as much as a blink of his eye he said, "You'd be no good to me laddie, I could never employ anyone who feels he is worth less than £1,400.00. Don't forget, we supply a house and car as well"

A swift mental U-turn and I managed to reply, "I'm glad that you said that, as I could certainly give good value for money at that level." I had just come through my first of many brain duels with Campbell, not realising that such jousting was one of his hobbies. Such a salary was to be prized.

"It might please you, Moira," continued Campbell, "to know that we have radio telephone in the practice. Each car has a radio and the base set is installed in George's house, although each vet also has a small set at home for use when you are on call. The system is run privately by a guy who works for the Ministry of Defence in Plymouth. You will be able to catch Ned on his rounds without the tedious chore of phoning through to the farms on his list. There are one or two blank spots in valleys, but it does save a lot of work and worry for the wives."

Moira and I had visions of second duty days when we could take the children out on the moor. This was a lovely dream but we soon found that being on second call meant that I would be fairly busy.

"Well here we are at your hotel and I shall allow you to buy Anne and me a nightcap each before we go home. Of course we will look forward to seeing you in the morning when you have made a final decision. I appreciate that we will not see you until the springtime. In the meantime I have made a cheque out to cover your expenses and have paid you a fair mileage to cover your journey."

Moira commented that she must be off to bed and bade our hosts goodnight. Anne and Campbell settled down in the bar and we chatted away affably in an arena of scotch whisky glasses.

Later, as Moira and I settled in our room I said, "Wasn't that a lovely evening despite our host being a bit different? What are your thoughts? Do you realise that the vet he got rid of was a second cousin of mine from Ulster? I have never met him but that name is uncommon! I wonder what the true story was!"

Moira turned in response. "I was watching you all evening, and my thought is that we should not turn down an opportunity such as this. You were very enthusiastic and it is right in your field. I liked Anne, who copes with a dominant husband and four rumbustious boys. She must be a very strong lady. Do you realise, she has her own toolbox to carry out all the d.i.y. jobs in the house because sir is always politicking? Working with Campbell will be a challenge at times!"

"I'm glad that you said that because I should like to accept the job. It would satisfy me professionally, and stretch me academically. I hope that you will settle here, as there is so much opportunity to paint in gorgeous surroundings."

We arrived at Greystones at 8.45 next morning and were welcomed by Campbell who was just going to the surgery.

"We would like to thank you both for your hospitality yesterday and to accept the position if the vacancy is still available"

"We would be delighted to have you join us. Ken Blake is due to leave us in the early spring and no doubt you will tell me how soon you will be available!" With that comment he swept away to the surgery, leaving us to say our farewells to Anne.

Moira flung her arms around my neck saying. "Just think how well things are turning out after our disappointment in the island. All this wonderful country to discover, and well away from the city's roar. Look at that sky on the moor. It seems to go from a beautiful blue to dark and foreboding in a short space of time. It is an exciting place of changing colours and hues. This could be the place to bring up our children."

The journey back to the Island flew by as we drove northwards. The excited chatter was unending as we discussed future plans and what we must tell our parents, who would be sad to see us leave the land of my birth and our large circle of friends.

Brian and Mary were so delighted with our good news that we had ended up in such a nice place and must have felt rather guilty as they had offered to pay for our furniture removal to Devon.

Back at work in the practice Mary stopped me as I was leaving the surgery. "Ned! Have I told you about my friend, Rex, the alsatian?"

"No" I replied, "but I get that strange feeling that you are going to tell me, and also that I am about to be roped in for something! Does it involve feminine wiles?"

"Sometimes I feel that you are quite distrusting. You are such a good vet and have this uncanny knack of handling wild animals. Rex needs a new home because he is a free spirit. He has scruffy little boys collect him and take him to the beach each day so that they can play. When he is left home with his inadequate owners, he is liable to corner them with lips curled until some one arrives with a lead, which of course, means walk time. He is so unreliable in the house that nobody comes to see them any more and they want him put down."

"Would you accept a challenge and help me train him? I have him in the spare loose box at the surgery and would really appreciate your help. Brian thinks that I'm being silly!

What could I say, except that I agreed with Brian. The following day, I was introduced to Rex who bounded up to me. He was a large brindle beast with hair going every which way. Certainly not a pedigree! He had been sleeping in the loosebox with Baska the grey gelding. The two of them appeared to get on well, possibly because Baska was over ten times his weight!

I quickly learned that Rex enjoyed relationships on his terms, and if he was not pack leader the lips would curl, and you could be in danger of being bitten. Mary walked in to the loosebox with a big raw beef knuckle joint.

Of course, Rex was overjoyed to see such a treat and sat when he was told. "Now!" said Mary, "this is where the training starts when I give him the bone." Leaning forward she put the bone onto the straw whilst Rex stood back. On the 'Yes' command he grabbed the joint and started to bury it in the straw, hidden away for a rainy day

"Now we shall take the bone back" continued Mary, calmly. "This is lesson one to show who is top of the pecking order. In Rex's viewpoint I shall have to be the alpha member of the pack if he lives with us!"

I was immensely impressed with her approach and said, "Where do I come in?"

"If you and I crouch quietly beside him the threats will start. Then we will talk to him constantly and quietly whilst moving a hand towards his bone. The other hand will be poised to thump him if he tries to bite. He now has two hands moving in slowly, from different directions, towards the bone. The dilemma is which hand to bite first, whilst this very soothing talking continues."

"You are slightly demented." I replied, with my eyes firmly fixed on Rex "but it is a great challenge to see who ends up in hospital first. Be aware! This is ninety pounds of aggressive dog."

"Keep talking!" was the response, "Your hand is bigger, therefore tastier!"

All the time our hands slowly approached the prized bone and Rex's lips curled and a deep rumble came from his throat, whilst we told him what a good doggie he was and we were so proud of him.

With my eyes looking straight into his my fingers eventually touched the bone, I slowly grasped it and rotated it, so that any bite was onto the bone. The threats ceased as he realised that he had been outflanked and was no longer the Alpha male.

Our eyes met and Mary quietly said "We've done it. I was quite scared but knew that you were my best hope! Now we have reached this stage training can commence and I hope that I can treat him like any other dog. I could use him to keep Brian in order when he becomes too demanding," she added, with a giggle. After further training Rex became a very acceptable member of the household. It's not what you do. It's the way that you do it.

After this little escapade I had a similar experience a few weeks later, when I called at the filling station for fuel. Gerry, the owner had a similar alsatian who was generally covered with sump oil. As he was in the garage all night as a guard dog everyone was accepted on his territory under sufferance.

Whilst I was there Gerry commented, "Bob has been a bit picky on food for a couple of days. Can you have a look at him?"

"Certainly Gerry! You hold his head and I shall check his temperature for a start."

As Gerry held his head I lifted his tail and inserted the thermometer. This was an affront so Bob tore his head free from Gerry's grasp, and grabbed my hand in his mouth. Somewhere a voice came to me, never pull away from a dog bite as they clamp tightly. Bob was really telling me, don't be stupid as I can really cause you damage. Gerry was very embarrassed so I said sharply, "Gerry! Hold him tight next time, as I do bleed when wounded.

We had another try and the same thing happened. This big dog was too strong for Gerry. I did not move, as he grabbed me with his mouth. Instead, I extended my fingers and rammed my hand down his throat. Bob let go, and ended up with lacerated tonsils. This was not in his rule book.

Next time I inserted the thermometer he stood quietly and let me examine him thoroughly. Suddenly, I had acquired the status of Alpha male.

During the build up to the wedding, life continued as normal and late one night the phone shrilled out just as we were going to sleep. John Kewin the telephone operator apologised, "Sorry Ned, they're out celebrating again tonight and I have a call for you even though you're off duty." One of the advantages of manual telephone exchanges was the social intercourse that took place. I could recall my mother phoning Jean McDowell in Donegal only to be told by the operator that Jean had gone off for the evening to play cards at the Gallaghers' but she would divert the call to their house.

There was a click as the call came through. "Mr Carson, John Cregeen here from Ballakilmuraugh. I've got some trouble with a Jersey cow. She's due to calve and leaking milk all over the place. She seems a bit out of sorts. She 'dropped her slacks' and appears to be walking about with her legs all splayed. A bit like a duck carrying a goose egg. Can you come and see her yessir? I don't like to go to bed, whilst she's in this state, even though you're off duty!"

I knew John of old. He was a semi-retired dairy farmer whose herd of 20 Jersey cows were all pets. Each cow had its own pet name and idiosyncrasies. This extended to the daily performance of calling the cows in for milking. They would all approach the milking parlour and then stand in a group about fifty feet away from the door. The only way that they would enter was for Juan to walk out, talking to them quietly, when he would scratch the head of Buttercup, and then talking soothingly and holding her left ear would lead her in to be milked.

As I arrived on the farm Buttercup was standing 'Bambi' like, in the yard with her legs slowly sliding away from her, until she finally became recumbent with her head laid back sideways, and milk pouring from her teats. All the symptoms of milk fever were present so without ado I slipped a needle into her neck and slowly administered the life giving calcium. After a couple of minutes she licked her nose and belched, life was returning. It did not take her long to perk up and the milk flow diminished.

"She's always leaked a bit of milk," interjected John, "Although it seems to ease off a few days after calving!"

"All the more reason to be careful John because she loses calcium from her body, as the milk leaks away. I think that you should have a look at her a couple of times during the night, in case this recurs and let me know in the morning anyway, for my own peace of mind.

I had a good night's sleep and arrived in surgery in the morning ready for a day's work. I was working out my morning round, when I was aware of Mary standing silently beside me, looking very detached and vacant. "Good morning. What a lovely day!" I greeted her, hoping to jerk her out of her stupor. "You are looking a bit pensive, too many late nights Eh!"

She gave me a long vacant –'there's nobody at home,' stare. "It's all very well for you. Mum and Dad arrived over yesterday so we took them out for dinner and sat and chatted until the early hours about weddings.

At 2 0'clock I was called out to a lambing. At 3 o'clock someone called to ask if they could give the dog an aspirin and to round off a pleasant evening, John Cregeen phoned at five-thirty to ask if I would visit Buttercup, who was showing signs of milk fever again.

I am not a happy bunny. By the way thank you for taking last night's call. We completely forgot that we were on duty. Now, I'm going for a cup of tea and I will make you one as a thank you. I told John that you would see 'Buttercup' later in the morning."

I smiled and chuckled. "Really, if the pressure is getting to you, there is still time to call off the wedding and remain an assistant." As she stumped out of the room she muttered something unrepeatable, so I felt it wise to set off on the morning rounds.

The first call, was to a small holding outside Castletown, to attend to a herd infertility problem. I had never attended Mr and Mrs Smith's animals before so I eventually found a small cottage half way down a farm lane which had a couple of small outbuildings standing out in the yard.

I knocked on the door and a little dark haired man dressed in grey flannels and of indeterminate age appeared. "Hello! Are you the vet? I'm John Smith. Please come in as we've just poured out a cup of tea and can discuss our problems." We walked through into a brightly lit kitchen and met Mabel, his dumpy little wife, who greeted me effusively.

"Do sit down." she said. We have been so worried about our girls, who won't have babies. You see we lived in Preston all our lives and after seeing all the happy cows in the fields, decided to live in the country in our retirement."

"How many cows have you got?" I replied.

"Only one, little Crocus, who is a very pretty Jersey cow and has now milked for six months and shows no signs of calving. The other two heifers, Ruby and Charlotte, don't appear to be in calf either!"

"How many times have they been served by the bull or the artificial inseminator in the last few months?" I continued, with concern.

"What do you mean Mr Carson? We haven't met these people yet. Who are they?"

I tried to maintain an advisory pose without smiling. Here were a couple of innocents in the countryside!

"The female cannot get pregnant without being served or inseminated with bull's semen. I wouldn't recommend that you have a bull with your cattle as Jersey bulls can be very aggressive. I believe that your best course of action would be to phone up the government office and ask if an inseminator can come out and talk to you.

There are only certain times that the cow can be made pregnant, so you must watch them carefully. When you see them riding each other, playing 'double decker ducks' they are ready for insemination. If they still cannot get in calf there may be other feed problems present and you should contact us again."

John and Mabel sat at the other side of the table with their eyes wide open at the thought of sex in the countryside. "Oh Mr Carson!" finished Mabel, "We didn't realise that it was all so complicated. We shall phone the government office right away. Thank you for being so kind." As I drove away, they stood at the door and waved me off.

I drove into John's yard sensing that all was not right. An air of dereliction was present, a broom lying against the wall, a bucket beside it and a few wisps of straw let down the normally immaculate area. The central dung heap was so neatly piled that John could have won a design award. John, dressed in immaculate boots and dustcoat emerged from the loosebox and greeted me in a very sleepy manner. His immaculate attention to detail even extended to nice pink hands and carefully tended nails. "Am I glad to see you Ned. Buttercup showed signs of returning milk fever, so I reckoned that I should stop the milk leak and tied ribbons around each tit. It certainly seems to have stopped the problem as she is still taking a bit of hay. Thank Miss Sutherland, will you for getting up early in the morning," he added with a twinkle in his eye. "I don't suppose that she will be turning out early after they get wed!"

I followed him into the loosebox to find Buttercup showing early signs of milk fever, and flaunting four large red ribbons tied around her teats. "It looks as if you've done the trick John, and she is on the mend. I'll inject her under the skin to stop it recurring, and replace the ribbons with teat bougies. That way you won't cut off the blood supply to the teats. Look at this high tech treatment. They are like stubby little pipe cleaners coated with Vaseline. I screw one into each teat opening and the milk flow stops so you can discard the ribbons. Only take half her milk each time for a couple of days and replace the teat plugs after wiping the teat end with spirit."

After making our decision to move Moira started her planning schedule. First of all we visited the library and read through any information available on Devon and Dartmoor so that we could arrive with some knowledge of the area. The next move was to investigate furniture removal agents and arrange the process of packing when the time came. Fortunately, we found that Mary had taken over this chore. The more we arranged, the more convinced we became that our decision was correct. As soon as the wedding was over we felt that we must depart, for better or for worse!

We were quite busy acquiring tea chests and boxes for packing our household goods. Many evenings were spent compiling lists and arranging farewell parties for friends of many years.

The next problem facing the practice was to arrange for a locum to fill in during the honeymoon which was going to be fairly brief and of course a replacement for myself! The locum situation resolved itself after Brian met up with Mike Kelly, a Manx man, who was preparing to move on to a university appointment later in the year. Mike had the great advantage of coming from a Manx farming family and, in addition had seen practice with Brian, so had a lot of local knowledge. He was also prepared to hang on for a couple of months if the assistantship situation had not been resolved.

During the next few months we saw a lot of Mary's parents, Mark and Madge, very down-to-earth Yorkshire folks. Because of their equine involvements we introduced them to Brendan and Nuala Rafferty, who were also members of the farriery fraternity. They got on so well and had many tales to tell of their own horse experiences. As Madge was very involved in wedding arrangements, we took a back seat and waited to be asked for help.

The wedding day arrived and we all gathered at the church to view the ceremony. Mark proudly walked down the aisle with Mary looking gorgeous in a traditional ivory dress to stand beside Brian. Brian looked striking in his morning dress and had enlisted his brother as the best man.

The reception was attended by their many friends and Brian and Mark managed their speeches with great applomb.

Moira and I returned home happy, but sad that tomorrow we should be opening another chapter in our life. Early next morning, we waved off the happy couple, as they flew off on honeymoon. I called briefly at the surgery to ensure that Mike was in control of the situation. He was fortunate to have Alan Ramsden, at his side to guide him over the hurdles in our absence. We called in to supervise the removal firm, and then home to Douglas to say farewell to mum and dad, before boarding the Lady of Man on her journey to Liverpool. They, of course, were so upset at losing us and their beloved grand children.

After arriving in Liverpool, we at once headed south through Cheshire towards Monmouth and the Wye Valley, which we had grown to love. An overnight stay in Pontypool with Gert and Bert, my mother's brother and his wife, and the next morning found us crossing back into England, through Bristol towards Exeter and Tavistock.

It had been a grey, murky day which, as we ascended the eastern side of Dartmoor, became more forbidding and the rain came in sheets as we passed Princetown and descended into the Tavy Valley.

Following our directions we arrived at Springhill Villas, to find that the removal van had beaten us to it and were already carrying our goods upstairs. We rushed inside out of the rain with the children to seek shelter only to find Campbell on his knees in the sitting room. His language was somewhat basic as the builders who had just departed drove in the final nail to retain a floorboard and punctured the central heating pipe. I recall that we carried out a repair with plasticine from the children's toybox and a roll of insulating tape.

A soothing cup of tea with children in our arms enabled us to settle down amidst the chaos of moving. Campbell did apologise for his artistic language and wished us a happy couple of days to settle in.

We had the foresight to buy provisions on our journey, so we could struggle through the rooms to arrange bedding for the night and feed the family.

It took two days to settle into our new house and explore the immediate surroundings. To our great relief, a neighbour arrived and introduced herself as Joyce Varney. Joyce was one of those truly practical Christian people, who believe that actions speak louder than words. She took the children off our hands to give us some breathing space until teatime. By that single act of kindness she created a friendship that lasted for forty years!

Next morning I called at the surgery to see William Cackett and prepare myself for loading my car for work. Moira in the meantime, went exploring into town and discovered the grocers shop, newsagents and Mr Dawe the butcher.

We were made so welcome in this delightful market town full of friendly country folk that we soon put aside our disappointment at leaving the Island.

Little did we realise the twists and turns of life which would face us in Tavistock. This was the place that I would formulate my whole veterinary career.

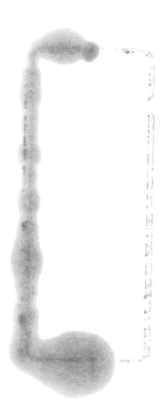